Acting Edition

The Mosley Street Melodramas Volume I

by Tom Frye

⃦SAMUEL FRENCH⃦

Copyright © 2008 by Tom Frye
All Rights Reserved

MOSLEY STREET MELODRAMAS VOLUME I is fully protected under the copyright laws of the United States of America, the British Commonwealth, including Canada, and all member countries of the Berne Convention for the Protection of Literary and Artistic Works, the Universal Copyright Convention, and/or the World Trade Organization conforming to the Agreement on Trade Related Aspects of Intellectual Property Rights. All rights, including professional and amateur stage productions, recitation, lecturing, public reading, motion picture, radio broadcasting, television, online/digital production, and the rights of translation into foreign languages are strictly reserved.

ISBN 978-0-573-66300-0

www.concordtheatricals.com
www.concordtheatricals.co.uk

FOR PRODUCTION INQUIRIES

UNITED STATES AND CANADA
info@concordtheatricals.com
1-866-979-0447

UNITED KINGDOM AND EUROPE
licensing@concordtheatricals.co.uk
020-7054-7298

Each title is subject to availability from Concord Theatricals Corp., depending upon country of performance. Please be aware that *MOSLEY STREET MELODRAMAS VOLUME I* may not be licensed by Concord Theatricals Corp. in your territory. Professional and amateur producers should contact the nearest Concord Theatricals Corp. office or licensing partner to verify availability.

CAUTION: Professional and amateur producers are hereby warned that *MOSLEY STREET MELODRAMAS VOLUME I* is subject to a licensing fee. The purchase, renting, lending or use of this book does not constitute a license to perform this title(s), which license must be obtained from Concord Theatricals Corp. prior to any performance. Performance of this title(s) without a license is a violation of federal law and may subject the producer and/or presenter of such performances to civil penalties. Both amateurs and professionals considering a production are strongly advised to apply to the appropriate agent before starting rehearsals, advertising, or booking a theatre. A licensing fee must be paid whether the title(s) is presented for charity or gain and whether or not admission is charged. Professional/Stock licensing fees are quoted upon application to Concord Theatricals Corp.

This work is published by Samuel French, an imprint of Concord Theatricals Corp.

No one shall make any changes in this title(s) for the purpose of production. No part of this book may be reproduced, stored in a retrieval system, scanned, uploaded, or transmitted in any form, by any means, now known or yet to be invented, including mechanical, electronic, digital, photocopying, recording, videotaping, or otherwise, without the prior written permission of the publisher. No one shall share this title(s), or any part of this title(s), through any social media or file hosting websites.

For all inquiries regarding motion picture, television, online/digital and other media rights, please contact Concord Theatricals Corp.

MUSIC AND THIRD-PARTY MATERIALS USE NOTE

Licensees are solely responsible for obtaining formal written permission from copyright owners to use copyrighted music and/or other copyrighted third-party materials (e.g. artworks, logos) in the performance of this play and are strongly cautioned to do so. If no such permission is obtained by the licensee, then the licensee must use only original music and materials that the licensee owns and controls. Licensees are solely responsible and liable for clearances of all third-party copyrighted materials, including without limitation music, and shall indemnify the copyright owners of the play(s) and their licensing agent, Concord Theatricals Corp., against any costs, expenses, losses and liabilities arising from the use of such copyrighted third-party materials by licensees. For music, please contact the appropriate music licensing authority in your territory for the rights to any incidental music.

IMPORTANT BILLING AND CREDIT REQUIREMENTS

If you have obtained performance rights to this title, please refer to your licensing agreement for important billing and credit requirements.

THE LOST SAMANTHA TREASURE

or

SHE'S BETTER THAN GOLD

by
Tom Frye

For
Samantha Kay Frye

CAST

MA FRYE – Heroine's Mother
EMILEAN FRYE – Our Heroine
EMILOUD FRYE – Our Other Heroine
CRISPY CRITTER – Our Hero
P. NEUMONIA J. HACKENCOUGH – Our Villain
MR. PINCHBOTTOM – Hotel Manager
ISREAL FRYE – Heroine's Father
STAGE MANAGER – The Play's Stage Manager
PIANO PLAYER/ BELLHOP/ PREACHER

THE SETTING

Turkey Droppings, Iowa. 1863

THE LOST SAMANTHA TREASURE was first presented by Patty Reeder and Scott Noah at Mosley Street Melodramas, Wichita, KS, May 25, 2000. Lights and sound by Marty Gilbert, props by Amy Saker, costumes by Patti Pfeiffer, musical direction by Steve Rue and choreography by Britt Hancock. It was under the direction of John Boldenow. It ran for 27 performances.

CAST
(In Order of Appearance)

LURISSA FRYE	Ali Spurgeon
EMILEAN FRYE	Lindsey Sutton
EMILOUD FRYE	Angela Geer
CRISPY CRITTER	Scott Noah
P. PNEUMONIA J. HACKENCOOGH	Monte Wheeler
MR. PINCHBOTTOM	Marty Gilbert
ISRAEL FRYE	Tom Frye
PREACHER/BELL HOP	Marty Gilbert

SYNOPSIS OF SCENES

Turkey Dropping, Iowa 1863

Scene I : The Frye family living room
Scene II & III: Train station
Scene IV & V: Hotel lobby
Scene VI :Hotel baUroom

Scene 1

(In front of olio curtain:)

MA. *(Addresses audience. She is carrying a small box.)* Good evening to you all. My name is Lurissa Frye and this is my story. It's not a long story, but one filled with lots of bad acting, bad scenery, and bad lighting. *(Blackout. She speaks in the dark.)* Sorry, you misunderstood. I said bad writing, not bad lighting. *(Lights come back on. In a whisper she says:)* He's a little touchy about his lights. Anyway, it all started about three weeks ago in my hometown of Turkey Droppings, Iowa. *(Audience reaction.)* Oh you've stepped there. *(Starting to cry.)* Well, I had just lost my husband. *(She grabs man's hand in audience for solace.)* No, it's okay, I found him in the bottom of the outhouse. You see he had fallen in. *(Audience reaction)*

What are you moanin' about, I'm the one who had to pull him out. *(Beat)* With this very hand. Well I meant to wash it, but I was too busy fixin' supper. As a matter of fact, the very supper you ate here tonight. Well, back to the real crap that happened. So my husband claims he found a map to the lost Samantha Treasure of Kechi, Kansas. Years ago in 1785 the Frye family headed West to make their fortune. Grandpa Frye settled in what's now beautiful downtown Kechi. He opened a combination saloon and fitness center. He named it Samantha, after his oldest granddaughter. He called it Samantha's Suds for Studs. It's amazing how good you think you look when you're drunk. Well the old man took all those profits and hid it in hopes that someday no one would find it. *(Looks puzzled at what she said.)* But he never figured that anyone would look in the bottom of a privy. Go figure. *(Opens the box)* Here take a look. That's it. Hold it up. Do you see where the big X is on the map? Well that's where the treasure is.

(She pulls a rubber glove out of her pocket and puts it on.)

May I have that back? *(Looks at person)* Well you didn't

think I was going to touch that did you? I told you where I found it. *(Looks at another person)* Well, here, you look at it. What's the matter, you Howard Hughes or something? So back to my story. I've got to prepare for the trip to *(Gags)* Kansas. That fortune-seeking husband of mine went ahead to look for the treasure. *(Waves the map)* Yeah you got it; he's one taco short of a combination plate. So now it's up to me and my beautiful daughters to take the map to him. This is where the story begins. *(Calls offstage)* Oh, children. Children. It's time to go. Children, are you through packing? My darling daughters, hurry up.

(**EMILEAN** *enters through the stage right carrying a dress and a wire hanger.*)

EMILEAN. Oh Mommy dearest, we're packing as fast as we can.

MA. *(Grabs hanger)* I told you, NO WIRE HANGERS EVER! Now, where is your identical twin sister?

EMILEAN. Did she not come out over there? *(Calling)* Sister dear, Mother is waiting. *(No response)* She must be in her room, Mother. I'll run and get her.

(**EMILEAN** *exits and we hear her running from stage left to stage right. She is behind the olio curtian.*)

MA. Is that you, daughter dear?

EMILEAN. *(Offstage)* Yes, Mother.

MA. Well, come out here, your twin sister and I are waiting for you.

(**EMILEAN** *enters from stage right. Hopefully, the audience will catch the running gag and think that the actress playing* **EMILEAN** *will be playing both roles.* **EMILEAN** *stands and smiles and looks sheepish.*)

MA. *(Continued)* Well, there you are, you naughty girl. We must begin our journey. *(Looks stage right.)* Now your identical twin sister has gone to look for you. I declare you girls will be the death of me. Since you were born I have never been able to tell you two apart.

EMILEAN. Well Mama, we did it again. I'm Emilean. *(Laughs)* Come out, sister dear!

(**EMILOUD** *enters from stage left. The two girls stand in identical poses and laugh together and speak in unison. Note:* **EMILOUD** *should be played by another actress much heavier and taller than* **EMILEAN**. *The more physical contrast the better.)*

EMILEAN AND EMILOUD. We sure fooled you, didn't we Mama?

MA. Yes, you did. My lovely girls. my Emilean. *(Kisses her.)* My Emiloud. *(Kisses her.)* Now you two hurry to the train depot.

(Girls glide together in front of olio curtain to stage left and **EMILOUD** *spins* **EMILEAN** *out of the exit.* **MA** *addresses audience.)*

Do you see my dilemma? Identical twins!

(Blackout)

Scene 2

*(**SETTING**: Train drop)*

*(**AT RISE**: All three girls are standing with their luggage.)*

EMILEAN AND EMILOUD. Mama, where's Papa? He said he'd meet us at the train station.

MA. Yes he did. I'm worried girls, Papa should be close by, but we know he ain't. Because of that outhouse incident, we'd know if he was within three miles.

EMILEAN AND EMILOUD. Maybe we should go smell for him?

MA. Good idea, girls. Emilean, you smell that way. *(She points right.)*

EMILEAN. Yes, Mama.

*(**EMILEAN** drops the suitcase and exits stage right.)*

MA. Emiloud...

EMILOUD. Yes, Mama

MA. You go smell that way. *(She points left.)*

EMILOUD. Yes, Mama.

*(**EMILOUD** drops the suitcase loudly on **MA**'s foot and exits stage left.)*

MA. I'll take the luggage to the hotel.

*(**MA** limps off stage right. **CRISPY** enters riding a stick horse from stage left.)*

CRISPY. Whoa, Periwinkle! *(Addresses audience)* Well folks, this is where I come into the story. That is, me and my ole hoss, Periwinkle. I don't like to brag, but this here's the smartest horse in the whole state of Kansas. Now, up there in Tow Peeka all they got is a bunch of smart asses, but they don't count. Anyway, I'd like to show you just how smart ole Periwinkle is. Periwinkle lay down. (**CRISPY** *drops the stick horse while still on him. Smiles.)* Good boy. *(Takes a few steps away from horse.)* Now stay, Periwinkle. *(Leads audience applause)*

CRISPY. *(cont.)* Now, Periwinkle will add for you and stomp out the correct answer with his little horsey feet. Periwinkle, how much is one plus one?

(We hear two stomps offstage. **CRISPY** *leads applause.)*

Good boy. Now how much is two plus three?

(Offstage we hear five stomps.)

Five, that's right. I told ya he were smart. Now here's a tough one, Periwinkle. How much is two plus two?

(Offstage we hear three stomps. **CRISPY** *smiles big.)*

Three, that's great Periwinkle, jest like I taught him!

(Beat and one more stomp.)

Sorry, he's jes a dumb animal. *(Picks up stick horse)* Now you go stay in the stable.

*(**CRISPY** throws the horse off stage right. There is a crash box sound.)*

Hey Periwinkle, stop that horsing around. *(Laughs at his own joke.)* Well now back to the exciting part of the story. *(Looks at woman in audience.)* Yes, I said exciting. Look lady, I saw who you came in with and trust me, this is as exciting as yer evenin' is gonna git. I sure hope I don't see that scoundrel P. Neumonia J. Hackencough in town. Why, that varmit brands all the women and kisses all the horses. *(Beat)* He's one sick puppy. Well, I best mosey on over to The Beacon Restaurant and git a plate full of grease, er, I mean grub.

*(**CRISPY** picks on an audience memeber in the front row. **CRISPY** brings the person up onstage.)*

Say partner, how'd ya like to help me catch that possum, P. Neumona J. Hackencough? It's a rhetorical question buddy, you ain't got a choice. Here's what ya do. I'm gonna hide through here. *(Points stage right)* Now as soon as you see him, you do remember what he looks like, don't ya? Good. Well you come up on stage and knock right here. *(Shows him where to knock).* You know, three times. That's the number right after two. Anyway, you knock three times very slowly *(stage left proscenium)* right here. Knock loud so I can hear you. Now don't fail me, or this stupid show won't be over til midnight.

(**CRISPY** *sits him back in his seat and exits off stage right.* **PJ HACK** *enters hacking and coughing. After boos he says...*)

PJ HACK. Please, I'm sick. Now, it's my turn to tell you the true story of the Lost Samantha Treasure. *(Note: here several things can happen in the script. If the audience member starts to get up on stage, he yells at him:)* Hey, you're not an actor; get the hell off the stage. *(If no one in the audience moves, the villain says:)* Hey buddy, thanks for not squealing on me. *(If the audience memeber knocks on the door three times,* **PJ HACK** *sits at the other piano and pretends to be piano player.)*

CRISPY. *(Sticks head out of curtain)* I said three times, stupid. One more knock. *(Hopefully, the audience member will knock again.* **CRISPY** *calls from offstage in a very sweet voice:)* Who is it? *(The Audience member should say his own name.)* Who the hell is that? Do you guys know anybody named *(***CRISPY** *repeats his name)*? Look buddy, we already gave at the office. Go away.

(**STAGE MANAGER** *steps out from behind curtain*)

STAGE MANAGER. Look mister, I've told you a hundred times, Lolita doesn't want to see you anymore. Now leave her alone.

(**STAGE MANAGER** *motions for the audience member to sit. After he sits,* **CRISPY** *appears.*)

CRISPY. Hey, what you find out? Where is he?

(Audience member should point to piano.)

Good work, now sit there and don't git up for nothing. Have you already done... *(Motions his head to the bathroom)* you know your bizness? Cause you ain't gittin' up and runnin' to the john in the middle of the big scene with the villain. Now, you just sit there and keep yer eyes peeled. *(Looks at the audience closely)* Whoa, what have you been drinkin? They're already peeled! **CRISPY** *exits stage right.)* *(offstage)* You're right Lolita, he's a babe.

(**EMILEAN AND EMILOUD** *enter from stage right and stage left, go to center and pose.*)

EMILEAN AND EMILOUD. Oh Pa, where are you?

EMILEAN. Eewww, I think he's that way, Emiloud. It shore stinks over there.

EMILOUD. No that's just this table. *(Pulls up same guy and leaves him on stage.)* They're from Oklahoma.

*(**EMILEAN** and **EMILOUD** exit opposite ways they entered. Hopefully, the audience member will go stage right to try and knock. As soon as the person gets out of their seat **CRISPY** enters.)*

CRISPY. Hey, hey, hey. Now, we're just not a very good listener are we? What did I tell you about gittin' up? *(Not letting him get a word in edgewise.)* Ok, now you're gonna need a time-out if you don't stop. *(He sits him down and exits.)*

*(**MA** enters from stage left and goes right to the audience member.)*

MA. Did you see my girls? *(Look for reaction from the audience)* Look fella you've caused jest about enough trouble for one night. Security. Security. *(An **ACTOR** comes up with a "Security" shirt and escorts the audience member out the front door with spotlight on him the whole time.)* You know its people like him that should go to see a Thunder game. This is a respectable place. *(Yelling)* And don't come back!

*(**MA** exits. **PJ HACK** enters and goes to woman with guy who has been on stage.)*

PJ HACK. Honey, you ain't missin' a thing. I'd dump him anyway; he's two-timin' you for Lolita. *(The audience member is escorted back to his seat.)* Now stay put. And any more trouble and we're calling Nola Foulston. *(**PIANO PLAYER** brings note to **PJ HACK,** who reads it.)* No kidding? *(To audience member)* Here, it's from Lolita. She wants to meet you at the usual place. *(**PJ HACK** resumes the play...)* Now if yer done playin' Bill Clinton, I'd like to get on with the show. My name is P. Neumonia J. Hackencough. Now you will hear the factual story as I told it last week on Jerry Springer. When I was born, I was a baby. *(Shows picture of him with baby body)* Wasn't I the cutest? *(Sappy music)* Anyway, I grew up a poor child of the streets. I had to fight for every breadcrumb and piece of escargot. *(Beat)* I was poor but I still had good taste. At the age of five, I started my first business. Helping old ladies cross the street. *(Maniacal)* None of them made it, but I always saved their purses. *(Laughs)* Then at thirteen, I enter kindergarten. There I organized the other kiddies into a gang, er I mean club. *(Laughs)* And that's what we used, clubs. Later I entered college at Wichita State University on a football scholarship. We had a perfect record, no losses and no wins. *(Laughs again)* It was there that I honed my stealing skills. So I worked my way up from nothing to Mayor of Kechi, Kansas. However that dolt Crispy Critter has halted my plans to turn this town into what every red blooded American wants. To be a landfill. *(Beat)* With a Kwik Trip on every corner. But if I can figure out a way to find the Lost Samantha Treasure buried somewhere around these parts, I'll buy up all the land around here and turn this place into a dump… oops, too late. *(Laughs)* Now you know why I'm a broken man. I just need a little love. *(Eyes a woman in the audience)* Will you love me, lady?

(PJ HACK goes to the woman and sits on her lap. He hacks and coughs into her napkin and returns it to her.)

Well, I have to go over to the hotel Eaton. I understand there are some beautiful women who just arrived on the 3 a.m. train in Newton. I must make them *(Smiles)* welcome.

(PJ HACK exits stage right, while CRISPY enters stage left.)

CRISPY. I'm back. I've turned over every rock and still no sign of our crooked mayor Carlos, er, P. Neumonia J. Hackencough.

(EMILEAN enters stage right.)

EMILEAN. Mother. Oh, Mother dear.

(They spot each other. Music plays "I'm Just a Love Machine")

CRISPY. Who is this booteous creature? Oh be still my throbbing heart. I must make her understand how lovely she is. Alas, I have no way with words. My mouth seems to stumble over every syllable. I stutter whenever I see a gorgeous creature like her. I cannot let her go without meeting her. But how? I know, I must have help.

(**CRISPY** *pulls another audience member onstage*)

Oh please, you think that guy had it bad. Anyway sir, you look like a stud. Well, maybe not. Anyway you must help me. You will help me woo this lady. I shall be Cyrano. She's Roxanne. And you're? *(Wait for name...)* Now you go over to her and say, "Lovely lady may I introduce myself?"

(He pushes the audience member over to **EMILEAN**.*)*

AUDIENCE MEMBER. "Lovely lady may I introduce myself?"

EMILEAN. *(To* **AUDIENCE MEMBER***)* Well?

CRISPY. Boy, you're good.

(**CRISPY** *waits for the audience member to reveal his name. If he gives his own name,* **CRISPY** *says:*) Not you're name stupid, mine! (**CRISPY** *motions for the audience member to come back.*) Tell her, "My name is Crispy Critter, you sweet potato." (**CRISPY** *pushes the audience member toward* **EMILEAN** *again.*)

AUDIENCE MEMBER. "My name is Crispy Critter, you sweet potato."

EMILEAN. Please to meet you, Mr. Potato.

(**CRISPY** *motions for the audience member to come back.*)

CRISPY. Well she's obviously not the sharpest knife in the drawer is she? Go back and tell her, "Welcome to Kechi." *(Every time the audience member starts to go back to* **EMILEAN**, **CRISPY** *grabs him and keeps adding more to tell her.)* And I want to welcome you to my town. *(Grabs)* If you every need anything, just holler. *(Grabs)* Oh, and by the way, there's a dance Saturday night and I would love to take you to it. Are you staying in the hotel or where can I reach you? *(Grabs)* Maybe you could give me your telephone number... as soon as the telephone is invented. I hope I'm not being too forward, but please consider my offer. You little cow pie. *(Looks at the audience member.)* Well, hurry up and tell her or we'll be here all night. (**CRISPY** *sees what the man does and reacts accordingly.*) Thanks fella, you've been a huge asset. (**CRISPY** *Helps the man back to his seat, then crosses to* **EMILEAN**.) Here little lady, here's my card.

EMILEAN. *(She reads card.)* If lost or stolen return to the Notell Motel.

(**CRISPY** *grabs card from* **EMILEAN** *and replaces it with another card.*)

Office of the Forest Service. You too can prevent Forest Fires. Crispy Critter, Floral Arranger.

CRISPY. Eh, that's Forest Ranger.

EMILEAN. Well, Mr. Critter...

(**PJ HACK** *sticks head in from stage right to eavesdrop.*)

...you can be the flame in my heart anytime.

CRISPY. *(To guy in audience who was just up on stage)* Hey, you could have had her first buddy but you move too slow.

EMILEAN. My name is Emilean Frye and I'm new in Ketchy...

CRISPY. Eh, that's Kechi.

EMILEAN. My sister and my mother came with me. You see, we're looking for my father. Maybe you've smelled him. His name is Israel Frye. He found the map to the Lost Samantha Treasure and he's out here looking for the treasure, but he forgot the map and we've brought it to him.

CRISPY. No ma'am, the only bad odor in town is P. Neumonia J. Hackencough. So you better stick close to me.

(Music plays Carpenter's song "Close to You," and they both do a take.)

Anyway little lady, I'll be as happy as Tammy Faye Baker at the cosmetics counter to walk you back to the hotel and make sure you're safe and sound.

EMILEAN. Oh Mr. Critter. My hero.

(Music plays "Holdin' Out For a Hero" from Footloose and again they do a take. **EMILEAN** *and* **CRISPY** *exit stageright to "I'm Just a Love Machine."* **PJ HACK** *comes downstage as olio curtain drops.)*

Scene 3

(In front of Olio curtain)

PJ HACK. So, do my beautiful eyes deceive me or was that the best thing to hit this burg, other than me of course. A fresh flower of spring. A Greek Goddess. An angel of beauty. I must have that little tart. *(Laughs and coughs)* She will be my bride. As soon as I find that treasure, I will marry her and then we will be as happy as Elizabeth Taylor and Nicky and Michael and Mike and Eddie and Richard and Richard again and John and Larry. All I have to do is find that old man before they do. Then I'll swindle him out of that map. Now it's over to the hotel and introduce myself and begin my tangled web of lechery and debauchery. *(Laughs and coughs, then exits stage right.)*

Scene 4

(**SETTING:** *Hotel lobby*)

(**AT RISE:** *Check-in counter with bell. Also table and 3 chairs.*)

(**CRISPY** *enters stage right with* **EMILEAN**)

CRISPY. Well here we are, Miss Emilean, safe and sound.

EMILEAN. Please excuse me Mr. Critter, I will go and bring my mother and sister down to meet you. I would ask you to go up to our room, but ...*(She's very embarrassed)*

CRISPY. I know Miss Emilean, it would be improper for me to enter the boudoir of a lady like you.

EMILEAN. I will hurry, my hero.

(**CRISPY** *blows her a kiss and she catches it and places it gently on her cheek.* **EMILEAN** *then blows him a kiss and it misses and hits* **THE PIANO PLAYER** *and he smiles and mouths, "I Love You Too'.*)

Bye bye, my little rice crispy treat.

(**EMILEAN** *exits stage right*)

CRISPY. *(To audience)* Well, at least I've met the girl of my dreams. I cannot wait to meet her mother and sister. I must think of some way to impress them. I know, I'll buy them dinner. We shall eat here in the lobby of the beautiful Hotel Eaton.

(**CRISPY** *goes to the counter and rings bell.* **MR. PINCHBOTTOM** *pops up from behind counter. When he pops up, he scares* **CRISPY**.)

PINCH. Yeeeeesssssss?

CRISPY. Yes, are you the hotel manager?

PINCH. Yes, I'm Mr. Pinchbottom. Manager extraordinaire. What can I do you out of?

CRISPY. Yes, I want to order dinner.

PINCH. But you must check in first. Let me call the bellhop.

CRISPY. But I don't want a room...

(**PINCH** *rings bells several times.*)

PINCH. *(Yells:)* Front.

(**BELLHOP** *runs to counter with bellhop hat on. He stands there looking stupid. Then* **PINCHBOTTOM** *rings bell again.*)

PINCH. *(Yells)* Back.

(**BELLHOP** *turns and turns his back to audience. Then he rings again and yells.*)

Side.

(**BELLHOP** *is not amused at this and* **PINCHBOTTOM** *is loving it. Then quickly he does several rings and* **BELLHOP** *does all the commands.*)

Front Side Back Front (**PINCHBOTTOM** *cracks up*) That always cracks my butt up.

CRISPY. I do not need a room. I just want to order dinner. So you can send monkey boy back to his tree. (**BELLHOP** *runs back to piano ala monkey hands and sounds*)

PINCH. Sometimes he just goes ape sh...

CRISPY. *(Quickly cutting him off)* Alright that's enough. May I just order dinner?

PINCH. Don't you want a room?

CRISPY. NO!

PINCH. Why not. We've got plenty. Prices are cheap. I've got just the room for you. It has a lovely view of Nafzter Park. Just last night three drugs deals went down and two drunks got rolled. You ain't gonna git that at the Marriott.

CRISPY. No, thank you. I've stayed here before. The rooms are so small that the cockroaches are stoop shouldered.

PINCH. *(Indignant)* That's a lie. I demand a retraction.

CRISPY. Ok, sorry, you're right. The cockroaches are NOT stoop shouldered.

PINCH. Look funny boy, do you want to order or not?

CRISPY. *(Put out)* Well, can I see a menu?

PINCH. Can you see my hand? *(Raises his hand)*

CRISPY. Yes.

PINCH. Then you can see a menu.

CRISPY. Look, Mr. Tightbutt.

PINCH. That's Pinchbottom.

CRISPY. Just bring me a menu and be quick about it.

> (**PINCHBOTTOM** *exits stage left.* **MA** *and* **EMILOUD** *enter stage right.* **CRISPY** *crosses to them.*)

Oh Miss Emilean, this must be your dear sweet mother.

> *(Both women scream and cackle.* **PINCHBOTTOM** *has re-entered and stands back with menu.)*

EMILOUD. Oh sir, I'm not Emilean. I'm her identical twin sister, Emiloud.

CRISPY. *(Stunned)* Oh good heavens. This is unbelievable. I cannot believe my eyes. The resemblance is uncanny.

PINCH. To who? Stevie Wonder?

MA. I know. I get them mixed up all the time. When they were babies the only way I could tell this was Emiloud was she would scream the loudest when I would drop the girls on their heads.

EMILOUD. *(Very proud)* Yeah, but now I can put a beer flat on my head and not spill a drop.

PINCH. She'll make some man very happy.

CRISPY. Please forgive me, ladies, I forgot to introduce myself. *(Proudly hands them his card)*

EMILOUD. *(Reads card out loud.)* For a good time call …1-900-77

> (**CRISPY** *yanks card away and gives her another one.*)

Mr. Crispy Critter. Foreign Stranger.

CRISPY. Eh, that's Forest Ranger.

EMILOUD. Wow. Forest Ranger. This is exciting. Do you know Yogi Bear and Boo Boo?

CRISPY. Well *(Blank stare.)* Boo Boo's dead.

(EMILOUD starts to make a face to cry.)

Just kidding. That's just a little forest joke. Where is you sister, Emilean?

MA. She'll be here in a minute. She wanted to floss her teeth first.

EMILOUD. Yea, I already flossed mine.

PINCH. What'd you use, a jump rope?

CRISPY. Please ladies be seated. I wish to buy you dinner.

EMILOUD. Oh sir, this is so kind.

(Women and CRISPY sit.)

CRISPY. Garcon. *(Snaps his fingers at PINCHBOTTOM)* Menus for the ladies.

PINCH. What ladies?

(EMILOUD glares at him and he quickly passes out the menus and hits CRISPY in the face. We hear a loud smack.)

Here.

EMILOUD. Thank you, Mr. Con.

(EMILEAN enters from stage right.)

EMILEAN. *(CRISPY rises and crosses to her.)* Oh, Mr. Critter, have you met my dear sweet mother and my darling twin sister?

(Women all scream and cackle.)

CRISPY. Yes, my pet. I'm so embarrassed. I thought your sister was you.

(PINCHBOTTOM offers his glasses.)

Stop it. Please, come and join us sweet pea and we will sup together.

PINCH. Oh really, well wha's up with you? *(Laughs at his own joke and they don't, he looks at CRISPY.)* Oh come on, I laughed when you brought them in.

CRISPY. Will you please just bring us all the blue plate special and be off.

(PINCHBOTTOM exits stage left in a huff.)

MA. Mr. Fritter.

CRISPY. Critter.

MA. My daughters and I are so thrilled to be her in Kechi.

CRISPY. *(Very honest and pointed.)* Why? ...eh, I mean, Kechi is thrilled to have you all here. This town needs two beautiful... *(Looks at MA)* make that three beautiful women.

(All three women scream and cackle.)

MA. Thank you Mr. Critter. My girls are not only beautiful, but you have no idea how talented they are as well.

TWINS. Please Mama, you're embarrassing us.

MA. Yes, you are my babies. They sing.

EMILEAN AND EMILOUDS. Mama.

MA. And dance.

EMILEAN AND EMILOUD. Mama, please enough.

MA. Emilean cooks.

EMILEAN. Mama.

MA. Emiloud throws the shot put.

EMILOUD. Oh, Mama.

CRISPY. Really Mrs. Frye, I would love to see them perform someday.

EMILEAN AND EMILOUD. Oh Mr. Critter, we just couldn't.

MA. Go on girls, show him how marvelous you both are.

EMILEAN AND EMILOUD. Mama, please don't ask us again.

CRISPY. Well if they don't want to...

EMILEAN AND EMILOUD. *(They scream)* We'll do it.

(They run to center stage)

Hit it.

(They dance to the song "Sisters" from White Christmas with lots of bumping and grinding.)

MA. Oh girls, you were just devine.

EMILEAN AND EMILOUD. *(They are now seated again)* Oh Mama, we love you, too.

(Once again, all women scream and cackle.)

CRISPY. *(Who is obvioustage left shell shocked)* My, my. Of all the acts I've ever seen, that's definitely one of them.

EMILEAN AND EMILOUD. Thanky, thanky, thanky, Mr. Critter.

(PINCHBOTTOM enters with four blue plates.)

PINCH. Four blue plate specials.

(He serves them. There is nothing on the plates. He goes behind the counter. Everyone looks at plates. Wipes their faces with napkins and rise. They make yummy sounds also. **PINCHBOTTOM** *then exits stage left.)*

CRISPY. Mrs. Frye, I hope I'm not being too forward, but there's a dance Saturday night and I would like permission to take Miss... *(Looks back and forth between girls and is puzzled because he cannot tell them apart.)* Emilean. *(Laughs)* Whichever one she is. And then with a reasonable time for an engagement, marry her and make her my wife.

EMILEAN. Oh, Crispy honey, it will be easy to tell us apart once we're married. Emiloud is the one with the huge mole in the middle of her back with lots of hair growing out of it.

EMILOUD. Oh yeah? You think that's something, wait till you hear about the hair growing out of her...

(MA quickly cuts her off, **CRISPY** *is stunned again.)*

MA. Now, now honey, we don't want to give away all our love secrets at once, do we?

CRISPY. *(Recovering)* Well, I need to get back to the forest station. NOW. I'll call on you Saturday, Miss... *(Looks back and forth again)* Okay, surprise me.

(CRISPY exits stage right.)

MA. Emiloud.

EMILOUD. Yes Mama?

MA. Honey, you go up to our room. I need to talk privately to your sister.

EMILOUD. Yes, Mama. *(Goes to counter and rings bell)* Oh, Mr. Bare Bottom?

(PINCHBOTTOM enters again from Stage left.)

PINCH. That's Pinchbottom.

EMILOUD. Oh, yeah? Well, we'll just see about that. *(EMILOUD strikes a sexy poise.* **PINCHBOTTOM** *runs off Stage left, with* **EMILOUD** *in hot pursuit.)*

MA. Now Emilean, since you're going to be engaged to Mr. Critter, I feel as your mother it's time I told you all about the birds and the bees. Let's sit down. *(MA is very nervous. They sit at the table.)* Now first...and this is very difficult for me to explain, but honey this is a bird.

(She pulls a picture of a bird out of her purse.)

And this is a bee.

(Pulls out another card with a bee on it)

You got that?

EMILEAN. Oh Mama... *(Very afraid and bewildered)* You make it sound so sordid and dirty.

MA. Well, you try spending a night with your father...eh, I mean, honey, that's just the way life is.

(PJ HACK enters from stage right hacking and coughing.)

PJ HACK. *(Aside to the audience.)* Well, well, well...what do we have here? A dainty little bird and an old bat. If I play my cards correctly, that little sweet petunia will soon be in my arms. *(Approaching the table)* Good day, dear ladies. May I introduce myself. I'm the mayor of this metropolis. P. Neumonia J. Hackencough at your service. *(He bows.)*

MA. Please to meet you, Mr. Hoopingcough. We are thrilled to be here in Kechi. But you'll have to excuse us, we must go up to our room and prepare for bed, it's almost 7 pm. It was nice to meet you. Come along, dear.

(MA and EMILEAN start to leave.)

PJ HACK. At last we meet. I hope I'm not being too forward, but there's a dance on Saturday night and since you both are new to town and don't know anyone this would be a great opportunity to meet people. I would love to take your daughter as my guest.

EMILEAN. Thank you Mr. Mayor, but I'm already going to the dance with my future fiance, Mr. Crispy Critter.

(They exit stage right.)

PJ HACK. *(Startled)* Fiance? *(To audience.)* Well, that little critter moves fast, don't he? But just wait until the dance. I'll show her my fancy footwork and then she'll toss him off like a prom dress and then she'll be all mine. ALL MINE.

(He laughs and then stops. Starts sniffing and cross downstage.)

Boy oh boy, do you smell that?

(All three girls enter from stage right.)

MA. Of course, that's my husband Israel.

EMILEAN. Yes, that's our Papa.

*(Olio comes in while **PA** is entering from the toilet after a flush.)*

PA. Oh boy, I wouldn't go in there if 'n I was you. *(Crossing through crowd)* Hey lady, smell this, it ain't that bad, is it? Oh look, there's my family.

(He gets on stage with outstretched arms and women run towards him and stop and turn quickly away. All are holding noses.)

Well, come here and give yer Papa a big ole wet one.

ALL THREE WOMEN. NOT ON YOUR LIFE!

PA. I'll admit, I'm a little ripe.

PJ HACK. Ripe? You smell like the north end of south bound jackass.

PA. Well as soon as Saturday gits here, I'll take a bath. What day is it now?

ALL THREE WOMEN. SATURDAY!

EMILEAN. Come on Ma, let's git outta here.

MA. I'm right behind you, cupcake.

PJ HACK. Don't leave me out here.

(All exit stage left)

PA. Well, now it's my turn. *(Looks at audience)* Oh come on, I don't smell that bad do I? (**PIANO PLAYER** *grabs his nose and runs off stage left.)* Anyway, I got reunited with my family and they brought me the map of the Lost Samantha Treasure. So now all I have to do is follow the map, dig up the treasure and my family will be rich.

(As he starts to exit stage left, **PIANO PLAYER** *re-enters with gas mask on.)*

Well, yer piano playin' ain't much better, buddy.

*(***PA** *exits stage left.)*

Scene 5

(**SETTING:** *Hotel lobby*)

(**AT RISE:** *Counter is gone. Table is center with two chairs.* **EMILOUD** *is playing Go Fish with an imaginary person.*)

EMILOUD. *(To empty chair)* You got any fives? Fives?

(Runs around and sits in empty Player 2 chair. Player 2 is very soft spoken.)

Nope?

(Runs back to her chair.)

Sixes? Got any sixes?

(Runs around to player 2 chair.)

Uh uh.

(Runs back to her chair.)

Sevens? You got any sevens?

(Runs around to player 2 chair.)

What? Can't hear you, what?

(Runs back to her chair.)

Sevens!...

(**PA** *enters from Stage left*)

PA. Honey, what are you doing?

EMILOUD. Oh, daddy. I'm so sad. The dance is tomorrow night, Emilean has a date and I don't got nobody. I'm gonna gouge my eye out.

(She tries, using the cards.)

PA. *(Stopping her)* No sweetheart, Daddy will find you a fool, er, date.

EMILOUD. Oh Daddy, do you think you can? Cause if you cain't I'm just gonna slit my wrists. *(Tries, using card on her wrist.)*

PA. *(Stopping her)* Now dumplin', Daddy always keeps his promise. You go get all dressed up for the dance.

EMILOUD. But Daddy, I ain't got nothing to wear, I'm just gonna suffocate my self. *(She puts card on mouth and he* *tries to pull it off. Finally he does.)*

PA. Boy, there's a lot of suction on that bad boy. Cheer up baby, Daddy will make everything alright.

EMILOUD. Oh, Daddy, you're the bestest daddy in this room. *(Hug and squeeze bit.* **EMILOUD** *keeps squeezing his face and yelling into it. She exits off stage right and runs around and jumps out of stage left portal and scares audience.)* Hey, we're gonna need a clean-up at this table. You pee-peed your pants didn't you. *(She exits stage left)*

*(***PJ HACK*** enters from stage left.)*

PJ HACK. Israel Frye, I presume?

PA. Now I sent that check in three weeks ago…the mail service is so…

PJ HACK. No, no, Mr. Frye, I'm not from a collection agency.

PA. You're not?

PJ HACK. No.

PA. Well, heck they're the only people that talk to me outside my family.

PJ HACK. Well, you did take that bath didn't you?

PA. Oh, I sure did, had to use sandpaper on my backside. I had a layer built up…

PJ HACK. Thank you. I get the picture. Please, let me introduce myself.

*(***PJ HACK*** hands* **PA** *a card.* **PA** *looks at it as if it's foreign)*

PA. Huh?

*(***PJ HACK*** sees he's holding it upside down and yanks it away and turns it over and gives it back to him.)*

PA. There.

PA. *(Looks at it again)* It's real pretty, but I can't read.

PJ HACK. *(Flustered and grabs it back)* It says my name is P. Neumonia J. Hackencough, Mayor of Kechi.

PA. Oh yeah? What's the J stand for?

PJ HACK. *(To audience)* Wouldn't he like to know. *(Cackles and pulls Jason hockey mask out of his coat and puts it on* *and then back.)* Why it stands for jovial. *(Laughs again)* Now Israel, may I call you Izzie? *(Doesn't wait for an answer)* Now Izzie, any man that moves to Kechi must play a friendly game of poker with the mayor. It's sort of a good riddance gesture.

PA. Don't you mean good will?

PJ HACK. Whatever.

PA. Poker, huh? Don't you have to gamble in poker like that evil city in Nevada? Lost Wages.

PJ HACK. That's right Izzie, you do. Why you're a regular hustler, aren't you?

PA. Well the only problem is I can't gamble. I ain't got no money.

PJ HACK. Well that's a crying shame. Don't you have ANYTHING of value?

PA. Wait a minute, I got a map to a lost treasure. That ought to be worth something.

PJ HACK. Lost treasure? Why, what a surprise. Well you can use my poker chips and use the map as collateral. What ya say Izzie ole boy, you game?

PA. Well, that's what they tell me. *(Puts armpit in **PJ HACK**'s face.)* But I'm not sure, Mr. Mayor. I could lose everything, couldn't I?

PJ HACK. Yes, but you could also win a lot of money, too. Then you'd have two fortunes. What do ya say?

PA. *(Stammers)* I, I,...

PJ HACK. Good. I accept your challenge. *(He shows him to the table. Table is full of poker chips and extra large cards.)* Now, sit down and let the cards fall where they may. *(He offers the cards to **PA** to cut. He does and **PJ HACK** puts them back exactly the way they were.)*

PJ HACK. *(Continued)* Now, one for you and one for me.

*(**PJ HACK** lays the first card in front of **PA** and gives himself one card.)*

And two for you.

(He snaps another card in front and then puts it back in the

deck and gives himself two cards.)

And two for me. And three for you.

(Same business)

And three for me. And four for you.

(Same business.)

And four for me. And finally, five for you.

(Same scheme)

And five cards for moi. Remember, jacks or better to open.

(PJ HACK *gives himself about twenty cards. He then fans out all of his cards and then makes a face like he has nothing.)*
Okay, can you open? I've got doo doo.

PA. *(He only has one card in his hand)* Yes, I open for ten cents.

PJ HACK. Ah, I'm dealin' with the Rockefellers, huh? Well okay, I'll call your ten cents. Here.

(He puts in a chip. He picks up deck.)

Okay, how many cards do you want?

PA. Four.

PJ HACK. Ah, got a pair, do ya?

(Gives **PA** *one card, but counts out four using the same card over and over.)*

Okay dealer takes three more. One.

(Gives himself four)

Two.

(Gives himself another three)

And one more makes three.

(PJ HACK *gives himself the rest of the deck, picks up the rest of the cards and fans them out. During the rest of the raising, he keeps getting louder and more animated and moves away from the table, throwing chips like a madman.)*

I raise you five dollars.

PA. *(Very timidly)* Five more.

PJ HACK. And five more.

PA. Five more.

PJ HACK. And five more.

PA. Five more.

PJ HACK. *(Kicking his leg really high)* AND five more.

PA. *(Beat)* Hmmmm.. Five more.

PJ HACK. *(Getting irate.)* And fiiivvee more.

PA. *(Quickly)* five more.

PJ HACK. *(Totally animated and throwing chips like crazy)* Annnnnnnnnnnd Fiiiiiiiiiiiiiiiiiiive Moooooooooooore.

PA. Two more.

> *(This catches **PJ HACK** off guard. He throws chips in the air and nearly falls forward. He recoups and throws one chip.)*

PJ HACK. One. *(Throws the second chip)* Two more.

PA. Five more.

> *(**PJ HACK** is all the way back stage left and throws more chips.)*

PJ HACK. And five more.

PA. *(Spits chip out of his mouth)* Five more. *(**PJ HACK** runs to the table like he's going to kill **PA**, stops, and sits.)*

PJ HACK. I call. *(Shows his cards on table to **PA**)* Read 'em and weep, Stinky. Four kings.

PA. Four kings? Hmmm I got two kings myself. Somethings smelly around here and fer once it ain't me.

PJ HACK. Why Izzie. You're not accusing me of cheating are you? That would just cut me to the quick, and they're ain't nothing worse than a cut quick.

PA. Naw, I guess not. But what am I gonna do. Now I'm broke. My family will never forgive me. This treasure and fleas was all we had. *(Holds up map.)*

PJ HACK. Tough nooggies, Iz, ole boy. *(Snatches map out of **PA**'s hand.)* Wait a minute, Izzie. I just got a brilliant idea. Tomorrow night is the big dance. What if you consent to me marrying your lovely daughter at the dance. Then all this treasure would be in the family.

PA. Well, I'd never make my daughter marry anyone agin her will. But if she agrees, it's a deal. Shake on it.

> *(They both shake their bodies and **PA** exits Stage right)*

Scene 6

(Curtain drops and **PJ HACK** *crosses downstage to address audience.)*

PJ HACK. At last my dreams have come true. Riches and a hunka hunka burnin' love. I can't wait to see the face of that dimwit Crispy Creme. *(He laughs)* He'll be dancing with his fiancee and guess who will tap him on the shoulder and say, "Pardon me skank face, but this babe is mine." *(More laughter and he exits stage left.)*

Scene 7

(Ballroom of the hotel/glass ball spinning and disco lights. Everyone is dressed the same, except **CRISPY** *is sporting a white tux vest, ala John Travolta. We see* **EMILEAN** *onstage dancing. Then* **EMILOUD.** *Then* **MA.** *Then* **PA.** *And finally big entrance for* **CRISPY.** *Dancing all to "Night Fever.")*

PA. *(They have crossed downstage right after applause.)* Aw Ma, ya still got it.

MA. I know Pa, 'cept now it's jest a little bit lower. *(They laugh.)*

TWINS. Oh Crispy, we had no idea you were such a mover and shaker.

CRISPY. Oh you ain't see nothing yet.

EMILEAN. Oh Crispy let's go git some sarsaparilla punch.

CRISPY. Oh yummy. *(They exit stage left)*

EMILOUD. *(She crosses to* **MA** *and* **PA.***)* Daddy! Where's my date. You promised me he'd be here.

PA. Now punkin', he'll be here soon. Why don't you go over to the buffet table again. *(Music starts again and she does another little dance as* **MA** *and* **PA** *watch in horror.)* Here honey. It's your valium tablets. Now, go on over to the buffet.

EMILOUD. Okay. Now, you holler when he gits here Daddy. Daddy, holler when he gits here. When he gets here you…holler. *(She crosses and exits and pops back out.)* Daddy? You holler when he gits here. *(Exits again.)*

PJ HACK. *(Enters stage left. To audience:)* Bite me. *(Crosses to Pa.)* Hey old man, I'm here and the preacher is waiting outside. Where's that babe of a daughter of yours?

PA. She'll be here soon. She's at the punch bowl getting liquored up.

PJ HACK. She better. *(Music starts again.* **EMILEAN** *and* **CRISPY** *enter from stage left and start dancing to "Staying Alive." Eventually* **PJ HACK** *pushes* **EMILEAN** *out and he* *and* **CRISPY** *start dancing.)* Look John Revolta. She's my girl now. I won her fair and square in a rigged card game. Just ask her old man.

CRISPY. *(Crosses to* **PA.***)* What?

PA. I'm afraid it's true son. But Mr. Mayor, this isn't the daughter I promised you. This is her identical twin sister.

PJ HACK. *(Grabs* **EMILEAN** *and puts her in a dip.)* Twin sister? You mean there's two like you?

MA. That's right Mr. Mayor. You can have her twin sister in marriage and then we can have a double ring ceremony. And then Pa you and I can live quietly ever after.

PJ HACK. Great. You git yer sister and I'll get the preacher. *(He goes off stage left.. **CRISPY** exits stage right.)*

MA. But Pa what about the lost Samantha treasure?

PA. Oh that, well Ma I lost that in a card game. *(**MA** starts to faint and **PA** catches her.)* Ma wake up, it's okay. I had already dug up the treasure before I lost the map to PJ Hackencough. All the money is in a bank in Toe Wanda. Now that we're gittin' the kids married off, I kin git you that double wide trailer I promised you and we kin park it on the Ninnescaw River and live in retirement.

MA. My hero. *(They hug and* **CRISPY** *and* **EMILEAN** *enter from stage right and* **EMILOUD** *enters from stage left.)*

EMILOUD. Pa did you keep yer promise? Where's my man?

PA. He's gittin the preacher now baby cakes.

EMILEAN AND EMILOUD. *(Squeal and jump up and down.)* A double wedding!!!

*(**PJ HACK** and preacher enter from Stage left. **PREACHER** stands center facing audience with rest of the casts back to audience. Starting from stage left to right the order is* **PJ HACK, CRISPY, EMILEAN, EMILOUD, MA** *and* **PA.***)*

PREACHER. *(Opens Bible and reads)* Dearly beloved we are gathered here to bury, eh, sorry that was last week.

Dearly beloved we are gathered here to unite these two couples in holy matrimony. Grooms do you promise to take these two women to love and cherish through sickness and in health til death do you part?

CRISPY & HACK. We do.

PREACHER. Brides do you…

EMILEAN AND EMILOUD. *(Yelling)* We do!!!

PREACHER. I hereby pronounce you husbands and wives. You may kiss your brides.

(The piano plays bridal music. First **EMILEAN** *and* **CRISPY** *turn and kiss and cross downstage right and then* **EMILOUD** *and* **HACK** *turn and he sees her for the first time. He screams.)*

EMILOUD. Oh baby you're mine now. Hit it, Mr. Music.

(Music begins. She and **HACK** *cross downstage left and Ma and Pa stay center. First dance segment is* **EMILOUD** *and* **HACK**. *Second is* **CRISPY** *and* **EMILEAN** *and last break is* **MA** *and* **PA**. *Then all dance on last break to "More than a Woman")*

The End (Thank God)

THE PLAGUE ON MADISON AVENUE

or

GENERAL HORSEPITAL

by
Tom Frye

For
Madison Lynn Frye

CAST

NARRATOR
MADISON AVENUE – Our Heroine
DOLLY AVENUE – Heroine's Mother
BUBBLES LATUSH – Madison's Grandmother
DR. BUCK KILL DEER – Our Hero Surgeon
NURSE RETCHED – Our Villain, played by a man in drag
DR. LECORIAN – Another Doctor
DR. STU RATBURGER – Hospital Administrator
GENERAL CUSTER – a Patient
MISS LUCE – a Pregnant Patient
MR. HINEY – a Patient

THE PLAGUE ON MADISON AVENUE was first presented by Patty Reeder and Scott Noah at Mosley Street Melodramas, Wichita, KS, August 2, 2001. Lights and sound by Marty Gilbert, props by Pat Szlauderbach, costumes by Patti Pfeiffer, musical direction by Steve Rue, and choreography by Tom Frye. It was under the direction of Tom Frye. The show ran for 18 performances.

CAST
(In Order of Appearance)

NARRATOR	Marty Gilbert
MADISON AVENUE	Megan Koppenhaver
DOLLY AVENUE	Ali Spurgeon
BUBBLES LATUSH	Angela Geer
DR. BUCK KILLDEER	Scott Noah
NURSE RETCHED	Mike Roark
DR. LECORIAN/ DR. STU RATBERGER/ GENERAL CUSTER/ MISS LUCE/ MR. HINEY	Tom Frye

SYNOPSIS OF SCENES

General Horsepital, Mucus, Kansas, 1871.

Scene I & II: Nurses station
Scene III: Dr. Killdeer's office
Scene IV : Hospital lounge
Scene V : Nurses station
Scene VI : X Ray lab
Scene VII : Operating room

Scene 1

(**SETTING:** *General Horsepital in Mucus, Kansas, 1871.*)

(**AT RISE:** *An old time western hotel converted into a hospital. Center stage we see a bar used as a nurse's station. Sign on the front of the bar reads, "This is a hospital so SHUT UP." Curtain opens to an empty stage with soap opera music playing. Over the music we hear the narrator's voice.*)

NARRATOR. This is a true story. Only the names, location, time and facts have been changed. The time is 11:00 pm. The beginning of the graveyard shift. The place is General *(Horse whinny)* Horsepital, 1871 in *(Clearing major phlegm)* Mucus, Kansas. We begin our story just as Nurse Madison Avenue reports to shift duty on the Intensive Care Unit.

(**MADISON** *enters and crosses behind station to inspect charts. From the opposite side enters her mother* **DOLLY**, *also a nurse.*)

MADISON. Good morning, Nurse Dolly.

DOLLY. Now sweetheart, I know we're at work, but I'm still your mother and you can call me Nurse Mother.

MADISON. I'm sorry Nurse Dolly, but we are nurses and *(Raises hand and puts other over her heart)* I've sworn "to uphold the dignity of the profession at all times, to live by the hypocrite oath and to be the best nurse ever to yank a catheter."

DOLLY. Well dear, I'm proud of you. Just think, three generations of nurses right here at General *(Horse whinny)* Horsepital. You, me, and mother.

MADISON. Yes, Nurse Dolly, but grandma, er, I mean, Nurse Bubbles, gives me reason for concern.

DOLLY. I know, but there's nothing we can do. Remember, she's my mother and your grandmother. We must try to forget her past as a dancer at Jezebel's.

MADISON. I'm so happy she gave that up and has taken up the honorable profession of nursing.

DOLLY. Yes, yes, but she still worries me. All those flashbacks she has.

MADISON. We must have hope, Nurse Dolly. Today the new doctor is due to arrive from Wesley Vet Clinic and maybe he'll find a cure for her terrible condition.

(Stripper music)

Oh goodness that's Nurse Bubbles now.

(**BUBBLES** *enters bumping and grinding and singing "Shake Your Groove Thing."*)

MADISON. *(Very disturbed)* Oh Nurse Bubbles, how many times must we go over this, "our uniform –"

BUBBLES. *(Cuts her off)* Yea! Great, ain't it. You won't find this in Janet Reno's closet. *(Laughs wildly, sees* **NURSE DOLLY**) Hello, Dolly! *(Cracks herself up)* Hello Dolly, get it? That kills me.

DOLLY. Now Mother, Madison is right. What if a critically-ill patient were to see you in that outfit?

BUBBLES. We'll they'll sure die happy. *(Laughs and shakes her thing)* Damn, I wish I had *my* pole.

MADISON. Grandma, er, a, I mean, Nurse Bubbles, you must leave before Nurse Retched arrives or you'll get another demerit.

BUBBLES. Aw, that old battleaxe needs to loosen her corset.

DOLLY. Madison is right, Mother. Hurry and take these charts to Room 222.

(**DOLLY** *hands* **BUBBLES** *the charts*)

BUBBLES. Hey, these are great charts. Those Gershwin kids wrote some great tunes. *(Starts singing the charts)* "I've got rhythm, I've got music."

(**BUBBLES** *exits.*)

NARRATOR. *(All these announcements are very hospital tone)* Doctor Spock, calling Doctor Spock, you're needed in ear surgery.

DOLLY. Speaking of doctors, have you seen the new one yet?

MADISON. *(Resuming her duties behind the station)* No, not yet, Nurse Dolly.

DOLLY. Well I have, what a hunk! He can play doctor with me anytime.

MADISON. *(Angry)* Nurse Dolly, try to control yourself, you're as bad as Nurse Bubbles. We are professionals and no person, no doctor, no man is worth going ga-ga over.

*(**BUCK** enters listening to his own heart with a stethescope. The part that you put on your heart has a big ear on it. He poises, then resumes listening. We hear loud thumping on the P.A. like a heart, then it changes to many different sounds as he moves it around his body. First a heart, then a very irratic beating. Now a train whistle. Now a cock crowing and finally, when it's on his stomach, a baby crying. He stops and looks very pleased.)*

BUCK. Perfect, just like we learned in Pre-Med.

*(**BUCK** now crosses to the nurses' station where **NURSE MADISON** sees him for the first time. She goes ga-ga, tongue hanging out.)*

Good morning staff, I'm Doctor Buck…Kill Deer.

(Deer in the headlights bit with spotlight)

And you are?

DOLLY. Hello Doctor, I'm Nurse Dolly Avenue and this is…

*(**DOLLY** notices Madison's tongue and puts it back for her.)*

…my very available, attractive and charming daughter, Nurse Madison Avenue.

BUCK. My, my, my what a charming woman *(Kisses her hand)*. I can't wait to play doctor with you. *(He chuckles)*

MADISON. *(Very goofy)* Ga-Ga

BUCK. Excuse, I don't speak grunt. *(Looks for help from **DOLLY**)*

DOLLY. Oh doctor, she's been working 18-hour shifts in the

OR. She's just a little giddy.

BUCK. OR? *(Looks to* **DOLLY** *for help.)*

DOLLY. Operating Room, Doctor.

*(*BUCK *is baffled.)*

That's the room where you do the cutting.

*(*BUCK *is still puzzled.)*

Everybody wears masks...

*(*BUCK *is still oblivious.)*

Where you get your highest fees, Doctor.

(The light goes on.)

MADISON. *(Composing herself)* Yes, please excuse me, Dr. Gorgeous, er, a, Dr. Hunk, I mean Dr. Kill Deer.

(Headlights bit)

DOLLY. My, doctor, that's such an unusual name, how did you ever get it?

BUCK. Well, *(Embarrassed)* my real name is Buck Bone Break, but I figured...bad name for a doctor, huh? What idiot would go into the doctor business with that name? Anyway, it was late one night and I was on my way home from emergency surgery. By the way, I got a standing ovation from my collegues.

MADISON. *(Very impressed)* Really? What happened?

BUCK. You see, I took the wrong bag into the operating room, and I had to remove a man's gall bladder with a nine iron. *(Laughs)* Little doctor joke. Well, anyway, I was in a hurry. It was dark, the lanterns on my buckboard were on high beam. *(Really getting emotional in the story telling)* There I was, speeding down this dirt road at nearly 12 miles an hour and there right in front of me before I could stop was...*(Choking)* ...Bambi. A young doe in front of a Buck. *(Breaking down)* I tried to swerve but it was too late. I looked up and there she was with that look of...*(Headlights bit...immediately is composed)* ever since that day they've called me Dr. Kill Deer.

(Headlight bit).

DOLLY. *(Unimpressed)* Well, that's 60 seconds of my life I wish I could have back.

MADISON. Oh doctor your story is so sad. But we must get back to work, patients are dying every minute. There's this terrible plague.

BUCK. As opposed to a good plague.

(No response by them to his joke.)

I see. What seems to be the problem?

DOLLY. Well, they just quit breathing and then they're dead.

BUCK. Are you sure, you're not a doctor? Well, who's the nurse in charge of this floor?

DOLLY. That would be...

(Ominus Music)

...Nurse Retched. It, er, she should be here anytime now.

BUCK. Well, I'm going into my office because the Buck doesn't stop here. *(Runs off quickly)*

NARRATOR. Attention staff, attention all staff. Doctor Zhivago will not be in today, he's out with the Trotskys.

(RETCHED enters, looks angrily at the girls.)

RETCHED. So I take a five minute break to go file my teeth and you two start loafing around.

MADISON. Oh, no, Nurse

RETCHED. Quiet. I will do the talking. *(Looks around and notices no music)* Where is my music? *(Appoaches* **NURSE MADISON***)* Why isn't my music playing? You incompentent ninny nurse.

MADISON. *(Very freightened)* I'm so sorry, Nurse Retched, please forgive me. I'll do it now.

*(***MADISON** *runs to turn on soothing music)*

RETCHED. You realize this means a demerit, Miss Goody Three Shoes

MADISON. *(Puzzled, looks at feet)* Oh please, Nurse Retched, in my entire career of nursing I've never had one demerit. This would blemish my perfect record.

RETCHED. *(Mocking her)* Oh please, Nurse Retched, in my entire career of nursing I've never had one demerit. This would blemish my perfect record. *(Hostile)* Listen, I've been in nursing over 30 years and no one but me has ever had a perfect record. Understand? No one but me. **(RETCHED** *starts to fill out a chart.)*

DOLLY. *(Trying to change the subject)* Er, eh, Nurse Retched, before you write up your report on Nurse Madison, the new doctor wishes to see you in his office.

RETCHED. *(Very pleased)* Oh really, he wants to see me? *(Takes out compact and check lipstick and reapplies)* Very well I'm going, but you *(Loving to pit the mother against the daughter)* Nurse Dopy must put the demerit on Nurse Madison's chart. Understand? And if you don't...

(RETCHED *laughs and exits.)*

DOLLY. That old fish face. It'll be a cold day in the morgue before I fill out that report.

MADISON. *(Pleading)* Oh mother, you must. It's an order. *(Near tears)* You cannot be dishonest on my account. Nurse Retched will ruin your career if you can't follow orders.

DOLLY. Wait a minute, *(Snaps fingers)* a great idea.

MADISON. *(Excited)* What?

DOLLY. I don't know, what we need is a great idea. Come on.

(MADISON *and* **DOLLY** *exit.* **BUBBLES** *enters.)*

BUBBLES. Well, I see Nurse Repulsive has been here. Listen to that garbage. She wouldn't know a good tune if it hit her in the mug. Let's change that channel from easy listening to sleezing listening.

(BUBBLES *changes channel to Rockin' Pneumonia and the Boogie Woogie Flu. Starts groovin'. Goes to piano and tries to climb up and on it. Curtain drops and from a portal enters* **DR. LECORNIAN***)*

Scene 2

(In front of curtain.)

(DR. LECORNIAN enters and sees BUBBLES.)

DR. LECORNIAN. Nurse Bubbles!

BUBBLES. *(Surprised and shocked)* Dr. Leprechaun.

DR. LECORNIAN. That's Lecornian

BUBBLES. I calls 'em likes I sees 'em.

DR. LECORNIAN. Come here. This plague at General *(Horse whinny)* Horsepital is getting out of control. Four patients have died already.

BUBBLES. Well Doc, that ain't too bad.

DR. LECORNIAN. This hospital only had four patients.

BUBBLES. Look at the good side, the staff is as healthy as a horse, and Nurse Retched is a horse.

DR. LECORNIAN. This is no time for jokes. I think there is a dreaded disease that is running rampant through the hospital. We must stop it. Our very careers are at stake, our very lives. I think there is someone on the staff at this hospital that is poisoning the patients. You must help me find out who.

BUBBLES. Well, first I'd check out the meals there serving.

DR. LECORNIAN. You think someone is poisoning the food?

BUBBLES. Honey, have you ever eaten hospital food?

DR. LECORNIAN. Have you any idea who would want to do such a horrible thing?

BUBBLES. You mean other than say these lines? Oh yea. I got an idea and she ain't pretty either.

DR. LECORNIAN. Alright, who do you think...

(DR. LECORNIAN starts to die.)

BUBBLES. Doc, you okay?

DR. LECORNIAN. Nurse Bubbles, I'm afraid I've been poisoned too.

BUBBLES. Man, you didn't go through the buffet did you?

DR. LECORNIAN. You've got to find …out…who

NARRATOR. Dr. Leprechaun, calling Dr. Leprechuan. Please report to the operating room, oh, and bring your step stool.

DR. LECORNIAN. *(Dying in* **BUBBLES***'s arms, gasping for breath)* Nurse Bubbles *(Almost a whisper)* I…I…

BUBBLES. What? What is it? What are you trying to say? Am I pinching your little Shillelagh? Oh doctor, doctor. *(She caresses his head and then suddenly drops him.)*

I don't know who did this but as God as my witness, I'll never go hungry again?

(Gone with the Wind Music. **BUBBLES** *walks off puzzled by what she has said.)*

(Blackout)

Scene 3

(AT RISE: Buck's office. He is holding a skull and appears to be studying. Looks at book, then to skull.)

BUCK. *(Begins to sing)* The thigh bone's connected to the knee bone, the knee bone's connected to the hip bone, the hip bones connected to the arm bone.

(He's quite pleased with himself. **BUCK** *puts skull away and brings out ball and paddle to play with. Play bits. There is a knock at door. The knock scares* **BUCK** *and he hits himself in the groin. Very high pitched, he answers.)*

BUCK. Yes, who is it?

(From offstage in her manly voice we hear **NURSE RETCHED.***)*

RETCHED. *(Low but sexy)* It's Nurse Retched, may I come in Doctor?

*(***BUCK** *composes himself. He walks to door bent over. He brings in* **NURSE RETCHED** *who observes his position.)*

BUCK. Hello, come in, Nurse Retched.

RETCHED. *(Looking down and pointing)* Maybe you dropped it over here.

BUCK. *(Returning and sitting at desk)* Please be seated, Nurse Retched.

*(***RETCHED** *slinks to desk and sits on it instead of chair. Puts leg up and adjust hose so* **BUCK** *can see her leg.)*

RETCHED Yes doctor what ever you say.

BUCK. *(He recoils)* Er, Nurse Retched may I introduce myself? I'm

RETCHED. *(Interupting and sexy)* Oh I know who you...are... Doctor Kill Deer...

(Headlight bit)

...and as Nurse in charge, I'm here to give you a charge. *(She's stalking.)*

BUCK. *(Very nervous)* Yes, well I'm somewhat concerned with all the deaths on your floor.

RETCHED. Doctor, I don't know why they all died, I personally did mouth to mouth on each one.

BUCK. *(Gasps)* Nurse Retched, what can you tell me about this lovely Nurse Madison Avenue?

RETCHED. *(To audience)* So that's the way it's going to be. Well, we'll see about little Nurse Madison and just how well she holds up under the thumb of Nurse Ima Retched. Before I'm through with her, she'll be in prison for murdering patients at this hospital. *(She cackles)* Well Doctor, just remember a young nurse like Nurse Madison doesn't have nearly the miles that a more mature nurse has.

BUCK. *(Under his breath)* Or the body damage. Eh, listen Nurse Retched, I want to get to the bottom of this plague thing. So you keep on your toes. That will be all.

(**NURSE RETCHED** *turns and tip toes out*)

There's something really different about Nurse Retched. And I don't quite want to put my finger on it. (**BUCK** *returns to his desk and pulls out a rubber glove, blows it up, and puts it on his head. Just then* **DR. STU RATBERGER** *enters. He is the hospital administrator*)

STU. Well, well, well. Working hard on your first day, Doctor?

BUCK. *(Unaware of glove on his head)* Yes, Dr. Ratberger. I'm preparing to go into the OR room.

STU. I see. Well I'm here to welcome you to General *(Horse whinny)* Horsepital, Doctor Kill Deer.

(Headlights bit)

As hospital administrator and former school board superintendent and fashion consultant, I want you to know that we expect you to work hard and not get too *(Looks at head)* cocky.

NARRATOR. Dr. Ratberger, calling Dr. Ratberger… you're not needed in surgery or anywhere else.

STU. *(Ignoring intercom)* Well goodbye, Doctor. Now remember it's not how much you accomplish, it's how many people you tick off.

(**STU** *exits*)

NARRATOR. Dr. Seuss, calling Dr. Seuss, your green eggs and ham are ready in the snack shop.

BUCK. *(To audience)* I must find an answer for this terrible *(Looks puzzled, runs to desk and looks up word, runs back to audience)* disease. I will find a cure, I will marry Nurse Madison and we'll live happily ever after or my name isn't Doctor Buck...

(This time no lights or sound. Finally, **BUCK** *exits and yells to spot operator:)* I hate you.

(As soon as he's off, the spot hits the empty stage and we hear the sound of brakes. **BUCK** *runs on just as the spot goes off again. He exists shaking his fist at the spot operator.*

(Blackout)

Scene 4

*(AT RISE: Curtain comes down and **MADISON** and **DOLLY** enter from a portal.)*

MADISON. Well Mother, have you come up with an idea?

DOLLY. Not yet, dear.

MADISON. *(Starting to cry)* Oh Mother, Nurse Dolly.

DOLLY. Now, now, honey, we'll think of something.

MADISON. It's not that, it's this terrible vision I had.

DOLLY. You mean like imagining your parents naked?

MADISON. *(Gasps)* Mother!!!!

DOLLY. Well tell Mother all about it.

MADISON. Oh, it was awful. It was like a bad dream.

DOLLY. You mean like this show?

MADISON. Mother, please let me tell you about the vision. It involved the new doctor, grandma, and Nurse Retched. I can see it all again.

*(Dream sequence for "The Good, the Bad and the Ugly" begins. Curtian rises, flash pots and lots of lighting. **MADISON** and **DOLLY** fade back into the portal as number begins. **BUBBLES**, **RETCHED** and **BUCK** are wearing sombreros, have long mustaches, and rounds of bullets draped over thier bodies and rifles. They do bad choreography to "The Good, The Bad, and The Ugly." After number they come back out and curtain comes back in.)*

DOLLY. Oh, baby, you saw it all, The Good, the Bad, and the Ugly.

MADISON. So what can we do? *(They whisper back and forth several times. getting more excited each time.)* So Mother, do you think it will work?

MADISON. Well, why did you tell me all that?

DOLLY. Because we had to kill time so they could change the set.

*(**DOLLY** exits.)*

(Blackout)

Scene 5

(SETTING: The hospital station. **NURSE RETCHED** *is at the front desk. A man staggers in dressed as* **GENERAL CUSTER** *with an arrow through his head.)*

CUSTER. Help me! Please help me.

RETCHED. Name?

CUSTER. Help. Help.

RETCHED. *(Getting agitated)* I need a name.

CUSTER. Custer, General George Armstrong Custer.

RETCHED. Yes, General what can I do you need?

CUSTER. I've been shot.

RETCHED. Where?

CUSTER. Please, I need to see a doctor.

RETCHED. Do you have an appointment?

CUSTER. *(Looking stunned)* Help me. Please.

RETCHED. *(Looking through book, casually)* let's see. I think we can get you in to see the docter a week from Friday. I'll just pencil you in. Now remember, if you cancel and don't call we'll have to charge you anyway.

CUSTER. *(He's dying and gasping.)* Can't, can't, can't.

RETCHED. No. No. Mr. Custer we mustn't say can't. We must be positive. *(Yells off stage)* Nurses Dolly and Madison get your buns in here now.

*(***DOLLY** *and* **MADISON** *run in and make over the dying man.)*

Take him outside, he's cluttering up my reception room.

(As they help him out, **NURSE RETCHED** *says...)*

RETCHED. Oh by the way, Mr. Custer, is it true you wear arrow shirts? *(Uproarious laughter, as they're dragging him off he yells)* Well, make up your mind is it a little or a big horn. *(Laughs again, looks at audience and is serious as she says)* So sue me.

*(***BUCK** *enters.)*

BUCK. What's all this noise out here? I'm trying to do doctor stuff in there.

RETCHED. I'm so sorry, Doctor. We just had a man come in here without an appointment.

BUCK. *(Aghast)* NO!

MADISON. *(Entering with* **DOLLY***)* Oh, Doctor, I must talk to you. That poor man that was just here needed help...

RETCHED. Now, now, Nurse Madison, don't clutter up the doctor's head with details. If a truly needy patient comes in I'm sure he will take time out of his busy schedule to help. Won't you, doctor?

NARRATOR. *(Frantic as all on stage pause to listen)* Attention all hospital staff: come to the emergency room immediately. Code Blue. Code Blue. Train wreck with 50 patients in the emergency room. All hospital staff. Code Blue. Code Blue.

(They all immediately go back to their conversations.)

BUCK. Of course I will, Nurse. Now I'm going back to lunch. If I'm needed, I'll be in the snack bar.

*(***BUCK*** exits.)*

DOLLY. Yes, Nurse Retched, it's my break time. I'll be taking a smoke in the TB ward.

MADISON. This is not a hospital, it's an insane asylum.

*(***MADISON*** runs off.)*

*(***LUCE*** enters.)*

LUCE. Nurse, can I see the doctor?

RETCHED. Can you see my hand?

LUCE. Yes!

RETCHED. Then you can see the doctor.

LUCE. No, you don't understand, I'm having a baby.

RETCHED. Really? Well come back when the doctor is in.

LUCE. OHHHHHHHHHH. I can't wait my pains are two minutes apart. Please, I'm telling you the truth.

RETCHED. Oh really? Well let me tell you something, little missy. When I had my first child I was in labor for thirty-seven hours. There was no doctor for miles. That baby was delivered by a blind farmer with palsy using a cattle prod. So don't give me any of your whinny *(Mocking)* "my pains are 2 minutes apart. Please, I'm telling you the truth." Listen sister, you can't handle the truth.

(**MADISON** *has reentered to see all this.*)

MADISON. Here, you poor woman, let me help. Nurse Retched, please, you must help her. I would, but I don't know nothin' 'bout birthin' no babies.

RETCHED. *(Finally resigned)* Fine. It's always up to me to save lives. Saving lives, saving lives, what kind of life is that?. All right, lady. What's your name?

LUCE. Luce. Miss Luce.

RETCHED. *(Looks at audience)* Naw it's too easy. Okay, this way to the delivery room.

(**NURSE RETCHED** *saunders off followed by* **LUCE**)

Hurry up.

DOLLY. *(Enters)* Madison, where is Nurse Retched?

MADISON. She's taking a very *(Whispers)* pregnant lady, to the delivery room.

(From offstage we hear a woman's scream.)

LUCE. *(Screams offstage)* I can't, I can't.

RETCHED. *(Offstage)* Ya big woosy. Toughen up. Now push, I said push.

LUCE. *(Screams offstage)* Oh please, Nurse Retched. I can't push anymore.

RETCHED. *(Offstage)* I'm telling you to push. Now shut up and push.

(Another scream from **LUCE**. *They come on stage,* **NURSE RETCHE** *is sitting in a wheelchair and* **LUCE** *is trying to push him across the stage.)*

Come on now, one more. You can do it. Now push or we'll never get to the delivery room on time.

(They exit.)

RETCHED. *(cont. offstage)* Push. Push.

BUCK. *(Enters while wiping face with napkin)* Hmmmm yummy. Was that Nurse Retched with a fat lady?

DOLLY. Doctor, that woman was *(Whispering)* pregnant.

BUCK. What?

MADISON. *(Whispering)* Pregnant, Doctor.

BUCK. Huh?

DOLLY. Ok, Doc, you've heard about the birds and the bees, right?

(BUBBLES enters.)

BUBBLES. *(Eyeing the doctor)* Well, SMACK my buns and call me a waitress. What is this?

DOLLY. Yes...ah mother this is Doctor Kill Deer

(BUCK does headlights, but the spot is about three feet off. He very subtley goes into the spot.)

Doctor, this is my mother, Nurse Bubbles La Tush.

BUBBLES. Please to make your acquaintance, Doc. *(Offers hand)*

BUCK. *(Very squeemish with her)* My goodness, Nurse Bubbles, that's a beautiful ring.

BUBBLES. Goodness had nothing to do with it, Doc.

BUCK. Well you'll excuse me, ladies, I'm do in the OR *(pronouced "OR")* room.

BUBBLES. Now, there's a man you can sink your teeth into, girls. *(Looks around)* By the way, I've been doin' a little research of my own on Nurse Retched and I think I've got an idea what she's up to.

(They quickly gather around her.)

I think she's been spreadin' a rare disease around to all the patients...well, when we had patients.

MADISON. *(Anxious and concerned)* Oh, Grandma, what is it? *(Music plays a few bars of Poison Ivy)*

RETCHED. *(Enters and sees Bubbles)* Well here they are, the three Nursekateers. And you, Nurse Madison, get to work. Nurse Dolly, you never put that demerit on her chart like I asked, so you're offically signed to the Leper ward. You can give them a hand in there, providing it doesn't fall off. *(Laughs)* And finally, Nurse Bubbles, you are out of offical uniform so you're fired. Got that? Kaput! Finito! Axed! Pink slippy! You're history, Babe. Now get out. I'm now going to see Doctor Bucky. Don't be here when I return.

(**NURSE RETCHED** *exits.*)

MADISON. Oh, Mother! Grandma!

DOLLY. Don't fret, dear, we'll figure something out.

BUBBLES. Don't worry kids, Granny has already figured it out. While you two have been helping the sick, I've been spying on the sicker...namely Nurse Retched. I know how all these patients have bit the big one.

DOLLY. What do mean?

BUBBLES. Well have you ever noticed that every patient has died on the operating table? Nurse Retched has been slipping the sick a mickey in their IV.

MADISON. Oh Grandma, how can we prove that?

BUBBLES. There's only one way. We must catch her in the act in OR.

DOLLY. But who? All the patients have died. There's no one to left to operate on.

(**MR. HINEY** *enters holding his finger.*)

MR. HINEY. Excuse me, but I have a hangnail and I wonder if someone could take care of me?

(They all turn and smile to the audience.)

(Curtain.)

Scene 6

*(**SETTING**: in front of curtain.)*

*(**BUCK** enters from stage right with hands raised for surgery.)*

BUCK. *(Offstage)* Nurse Retched, come out here please, I'm sterile now.

*(**NURSE RETCHED** enters with rubber gloves and masks.)*

RETCHED. Yes, Doctor. Let me help you.

*(**BUCK** sneezes into his hands and then holds them for her to put gloves on.)*

BUCK. Very stange that a patient would arrive and need surgery in the middle of my golf game. Do you have his x-rays?

RETCHED. Yes, Doctor. *(**NURSE RETCHED** hands him x-rays with a big X on it.)*

BUCK. Interesting, Nurse Retched. What do you make of it?

RETCHED. *(With glee)* Well, I'd say he needs some major cuttin', doc. *(Aside)* And while the patient is on the table, I'll see to it that Nurse Madison hands the doctor the wrong instruments and then he'll think she's the murderer. *(Laughs)*

BUCK. Very well, let's go to the OR room. I love performing surgery in front of such a gallery of spectators.

*(**BUCK** starts to shake audiences hands. Finally **RETCHED** drags him off stage left.)*

Scene 7

(Nurses' station with **MR. HINEY** *on the bar and sheet over him. Other nurses have masks on already.* **BUCK** *and* **NURSE RETCHED** *enter)*

BUCK. *(Screams when he sees nurses)* Oh my God, it's a holdup. *(Raises hands)*

RETCHED. Doctor, they're just prepared for surgery.

BUCK. I knew that. What do you take me for, a ninny? Now first, nurses, good bedside manners. (**BUCK** *goes to operating table. He takes out a napkin and puts it under his chin.)* Would you pass the potatoes, please?

MR. HINEY. Surgery? I don't think I need sur…

BUCK. SHUT UP. I'm the doctor. *(Looks at* **NURSE RETCHED***)* I am the doctor aren't I?

(**NURSE RETCHED** *nods "yes")*

Now don't be frightened Mr…Mr. ?

MR. HINEY. Hiney, Doctor.

BUCK. No, I'm not a hiney doctor… although I do enjoy pinching a nice firm…

MADISON. His name is Mr. Hiney, Buck

BUCK. Of course. Now, Mr. Hineybuck.

DOLLY. Gas, doctor? *(Holding ether mask)*

BUCK. Yes. *(Rubbing stomach)* I just can't eat at Taco Bell.

RETCHED. *(Whispering to* **BUCK***)* Doctor, I believe Nurse Madison is responsible for all the deaths in surgery. Watch her carefully. If she hands you the wrong instrument, then she's the killer.

BUBBLES. *(Whispering to* **BUCK***)* Doctor, I believe Nurse Retched is responsible for all the deaths in surgery. Watch her carefully. If she hands you the wrong IV bag, then she's the killer.

BUCK. *(Aside to the audience)* They all must think I'm a nincompoop to not realize that there's something smelly going on in this room.

(All nurses lean back and look behind **BUCK***)*

BUCK. *(continued)* Just you watch a wizard at work. I'll solve this mystery or my name isn't Doctor Kill Deer... *(Headlights bit)* ...for nothing. *(Back to surgery)* All right, let's get to cuttin'.

MR. HINEY. Wait, Doc. Aren't you going to put me out?

BUCK. Antistetic, nurse.

(NURSE RETCHED pulls out a big hammer.)

MR. HINEY. Never mind, I brought a bullet.

RETCHED. Doctor, do you want me to start the IV? *(Indicating pole)*

BUCK. That would be nice, but let's talk about gardening later, Nurse Retched.

RETCHED. No, Doctor, I mean the IV. You know. *(Points to pole)*

BUCK. Oh, yes, by all means. Fill 'er up. *(NURSE RETCHED is hooking up the pole and switches bag so you can't see label. Meanwhile, BUCK is picking teeth with his hands.)* Ready? *(Soap opera music begins and everyone including MR. HINEY look to see where it's coming from.)* Scalpel.

MADISON. Scalpel *(Hands big knife to BUBBLES)*

BUBBLES. Scalpel *(Hands it to DOLLY)*

DOLLY. Scalpel *(Hands to RETCHED)*

RETCHED. Scalpel *(Hands big knife to BUCK and it cuts him)*

BUCK. AHHH.

RETCHED. Sorry, Doctor.

BUCK. Tongs

MADISON. Tongs

BUBBLES. Tongs

DOLLY. Tongs

RETCHED. Tongs

(BUCK uses tongs and sends them back.)

BUCK. Tongs

RETCHED. Tongs

DOLLY. Tongs

BUBBLES. Tongs

MADISON. Tongs *(Still holding tongs)*

BUCK. Wallet

*(**MADISON** rolls **MR. HINEY** on his side and uses tongs to take his wallet.)*

MADISON. Wallet.

(Hands tongs and wallet down the line.)

BUBBLES. Wallet

DOLLY. Wallet

RETCHED. Wallet

*(**BUCK** puts wallet in his pocket.)*

BUCK. *(Aside)* This will be the test if Nurse Madison is the killer. Defibulator *(Retched has snuck around and from under table hands up ping pong paddles.)*

MADISON. *(Looking at them very puzzled)* Difibulator *(Each nurse does the same.)*

BUBBLES. Difibulator

DOLLY. Difibulator

RETCHED. Difibulator *(Smiling)*

BUCK. *(Receiving paddles)* This is not a difibulator. *(Suspiciously)* Nurse Madison, I could have killed this man with these.

*(**BUBBLES** has gone around and has IV pole where everyone can see it.)*

BUBBLES. Not as quickly as giving him an IV filled with *(Turns bag to reveal it says KOOL-AID)* this. *(She looks at it carefully.)* And it's grape too.

DOLLY. That's right, Doctor. You wanted a difibulator. And what is a difibulator? But Paddles, right? And these are paddles. So technically, Nurse Madison is right.

*(They all look at **BUCK**.)*

BUBBLES. Doctor, I've been following Nurse Retched for months. I suspected that it was she who has been killing all our patients.

*(**NURSE RETCHED** grabs huge syringe over **MR. HINEY** on table.)*

RETCHED. Stand back, or he gets it right in the gizzard.

BUCK. *(To other nurses)* Now, is that an organ?

(**BUBBLES** *pulls out gun.*)

BUBBLES. Put down that syringe.

(**RETCHED** *does. In* **MR. HINEY.** *He sits up and staggers.*)

MR. HINEY. Ohhhhhhhhh.

(**MR. HINEY** *dies offstage.*)

BUCK. Oh Nurse Madison, how could I have suspected you?

MADISON. *(Looking offstage)* Poor Mr. Hiney.

BUCK. Hellooooo, I'm apologizing here.

MADISON. But that dear man...he ...

BUCK. Look, if it makes you feel any better, the operation is on the house. Now look, everyone is happy. We've found the killer and there's still time for one more thing.

MADISON. Oh Buck, do you mean?

BUCK. Yes. I can just get in 18 holes before dark

DOLLY. Mom, why did you suspect Nurse Retched?

BUBBLES. Because we've been rivals for years.

MADISON. You mean in nursing school?

BUBBLES. No. When I was at Jezebel's, she was at Michelle's Beach House.

(**NURSE RETCHED** *turns and is reading Moby Dick.*)

The End

COSTUME PLOT

NURSE MADISON & NURSE DOLLY. White nursing uniform. Hat, shoes, white hose, etc.

NURSE RETCHED. Same as other two. Also short white cape.

DOCTOR BUCK. All in white.

BUBBLES. Like Madison and Dolly, except very sexy. Sequins, Slit up the side of the dress, fringe, tassles. Sleezy.

DR. LECORIAN. Green jacket

CUSTER. Long hair, frings coat, hoots, and Custer hat.

MR. HINEY. Whatever.

MISS LUCE. Pregnant outfit.

DR. STU RATBERGER. Very tacky coat and Hitler mustache.

THE MYSTERY OF BABY LEAH

or

SHE'S MY RAE OF SUNSHINE

by
Tom Frye

*For
Leah Rae Frye*

CAST

PEARL – Pregnant waif
3 WISE MEN – Can be doubled with other characters
PIANO PLAYER – No lines
JOHNNY RINGO – Our cowboy hero
MA RINGO – Old farm woman
BILLY BOY – Johnny's very flamboyant brother
JUDGE NASTY – Our villian
CHIEF SMOKEINCRACK – Chief of indians
GREATER TUNA – A brave
LITTLE BEAVER – A brave
RUBY – Our mute heroine

THE MYSTERY OF BABY LEAH

THE MYSTERY OF BABY LEAH was fIrst presented by Patty Reeder and Scott Noah at Mosley Street Melodramas, Wichita, KS, April 3, 2003. Lights and sound by Marty Gilbert, props by Pat Szlauderbach, Costumes by Patty Reeder, musical direction by Larry Jensen, and choreography by Jenna Tyrell. It was under the direction of Tom Frye. The show ran for 24 performances.

CAST
(In Order of Appearance)

NARRATOR	Tom Frye
PEARL GOLDBERG	Karen Robu
THREE WISE MEN	Jeff Gates, Scott Noah & Randy Ervin
JOHNNY RINGO	Nathan Houseman
MA RINGO	Bambi Stofer
JUDGE NASTY	Jeff Gates
BILLY BOY	Scott Noah
RUBY SLIPPERS	Jenna Tyrell
CHIEF SMOKENCRACK	Randy Ervin
GREATER TUNA	Tom Frye
LITTLE BEAVER	Marty' Gilbert

SYNOPSIS OF SCENES

Kansas Territory 1880's

Scene I (In a snow storm on the plains)
Scene II (The Ringo farm house)
Scene III (Somewhere on the prairie)
Scene IV (Around the covered wagon on the prairie)
Scene V (Judge Nasty's cabin)

Scene 1

*(**AT RISE:** The **NARRATOR** starts in front of curtain in a spotlight and moves stage right.)*

NARRATOR. This story begins many years ago in the Kansas Territory. It's not a pretty story, but then neither are the actors. But none the less, it has to be told. It's really a mystery. The mystery of baby Leah. But I'm getting ahead of myself, let's start at the beginning so you know exactly what happened.

(The curtain rises on an dark stage. Outdoor set. We hear the distinct sound of a terrible snow storm. Sad music played throughout.)

Picture this, a young woman, wearing a tattered dress.

*(Lights come up on stage. **PEARL** is upstage right.)*

She is freezing.

*(**PEARL** shivers.)*

She is bewildered.

*(**PEARL** looks stupidly at the audience.)*

The blinding snow and wind are making her footsteps near impossible.

*(**PEARL** is stage left slowly making her way to stage right.)*

And even worse...

(Music builds.)

....she is with child.

*(**PEARL** opens shawl and points to stomach.)*

It's bitter cold. Colder than a witches...

(Music abruptly stops.)

PEARL. *(Glaring at him.)* Eh, eh, eh! This is a family show.

NARRATOR. Ok, ok.

(Music begins again.)

With each step the snow is driving her back.

PEARL. Oh, won't someone help me?

(Each time she reaches stage right a hand full of snow hits her in the face and she falls back to center stage and tries again

very slowly.)

NARRATOR. Her very life is in danger. Not to mention that of her unborn child. Folks, it don't look good. This story is even more tragic than voting in Florida. Could anything else happen to this poor woman? *(Music stops again.)*

PEARL. *(Breaks character, crosses to stage right and addresses* **NARRATOR.***)* Oh, not a thing! You try retaining water for nine months, and puking your guts out every morning while your husband is snoring away. Oh and let's not forget trying to get in and out of the bathtub when you're the size of a HIPPOPOTAMUS. And the pain in my back has only been constant for about...oh...let's say...THREE MONTHS! And would you like to talk about STRETCH MARKS?! Men, they love to party, but never stay around for the clean up.

*(***PEARL** *storms back to her position on stage in a huff and resumes pose as the worn out traveler. She yells at the piano player.)*

Hey, Billy Joel, what are you looking at? Play already.

(He jumps and starts playing again.)

NARRATOR. Well...eh...at least you're glowing.

*(***PEARL** *quickly turns and glares at him.)*

Yeah...well, our young woman seems to be on her last gasp of breath...

PEARL. *(She looks to the heavens.)* There it is. That same bright star I've been following all night. But I can't go on. This is where I will perish for sure. *(She is starting to fall.)*

NARRATOR. And then suddenly, from out of nowhere, it looked like help had arrived. She couldn't believe her eyes. Coming through the storm was surely to be her salvation.

(Music fades into "We Three Kings." Entering stage right through the tossing snow, are the **THREE WISE MEN**, *three actors dressed in Wise Men garb. They do not notice* **PEARL** *but are having a discussion about the star and where they're*

going.)

1ST MAN. No, No, No, I don't need a roadmap. It's only been ten days. I can find it.

2ND MAN. Well, I hope we make it by Christmas.

1ST MAN: Speaking of Christmas, what gift did you bring? I've brought Gold.

2ND MAN. I'm bringing Frankenscence. *(He shows them.)*

3RD MAN. *(Smiling)* I'm bringing Cheeze Whiz and little Weenies.

*(They exit stage right as **PEARL** stands in amazement.)*

PEARL. *(Yelling as they leave)* Hey, what are you? A bunch of wise guys?

(Sad music resumes.)

NARRATOR. Anyway. She decided now was the time to make peace with her maker. She knelt to pray.

(She glares at the narrator with contempt. Music stops.)

She STOOD to pray. As her eyes filled with tears and her heart with sadness, she heard a sound in the distance.

*(Hero music. Entering stage right, dressed in typical cowboy garb, with white hat, is **JOHNNY**. He is riding a stick horse with jam box attached to it. He rides down to center stage and doesn't notice **PEARL**.)*

JOHNNY. Boy! *(To audience:)* Howdy! *(Audience will probably reply. When they do, he looks puzzled and realizes their mistake.)* No! That's the name of the group. Boy Howdy!

(Boy Howdy song is playing and he shuts it off.) Well, I'll be doggone if this ain't the worst snow storm I've ever seen. Anyone caught out here on foot would freeze to death. I better get home fast before Ma starts to worry. Besides, ole Buck here is needen a warm stall and some oats.

*(**JOHNNY** circles stage left around Pearl and heads off stage right. Again Pearl is baffled. A few seconds later he rides back on again and crosses down center stage. He looks at her as she poses sadly. Sad music begins. He addresses the audience.)*

JOHNNY. Does that little lady look like she's in trouble to you?

(He looks back and she reveals her stomach. Music stops.)

Whoa! DOUBLE TROUBLE.

(JOHNNY crosses to her and removes his hat.)

Howdy little, eh, I mean, Lady. Are you all right?

PEARL. Why of course cowboy. I'm just out here making snow angels.

(JOHNNY smiles. She yells.)

You big schmuck. Of course I'm not alright. I'm standing here in the middle of a snow storm with no coat or hat and I'm freezing my touchus off.

(JOHNNY pauses and puts his hat on her.)

Oh gee thanks, that helps. Who are you?

("Hava Nagila" music)

The Shalom Ranger? This is where you put me on your horse and take me to shelter.

JOHNNY. Oh, I'm not sure, ya see Buck doesn't like strangers riding on him

PEARL. *(Yelling)* Put me on that horse now you big pile of cow chips. *(She gets on.)* Now make dust, Goober.

(Music plays "Lone Ranger Theme". They ride off and curtain falls.)

NARRATOR. Well as you can see, the time of delivery was drawing near, our mother to be was just a bit unpleasant to be around.

(PEARL quickly sticks her head in from stage right and glares at NARRATOR.)

Eh, but with good reason, because men are pigs.

(PEARL grins and disappears.)

So our hero took our beautiful expectant mother back to his homestead. To a warm and caring home that he shared with his mother and kid brother. But questions were still unanswered. Who is this mystery woman?

(Mystery music.)

NARRATOR. *(Continued)* Why is she stranded in a snowstorm?

(Mystery music)

And who is the father of her baby?

(Mystery music)

And now ladies and gentlemen, for your curiosity, The Mystery of Baby Leah or She's My Rae of Sunshine.

(Blackout)

Scene 2

(**SETTING:** *Interior of a house in 1880's Kansas. Table and two chairs*)

(*Hero music.* **JOHNNY** *enters from stage right.*)

JOHNNY. It's alright. Ma must be in the kitchen. Come on in.

PEARL. (*Entering stage right*) Oh, I'm so scared and all alone. I don't even know your name, stranger. What must you think of me.

JOHNNY. (*Taking off his hat*) No, ma'am. It's me that ought to be feelin' bad. I haven't properly introduced myself. My name is Johnny Ringo.

(*"Ta Da" music*)

Welcome to our home. And what might your name be, pretty lady?

PEARL. (*Soft and coy*) Why, my name is Pearl. (*Smiles*) Pearl Goldberg.

JOHNNY. Pearl. What a jewel of a name. Beautiful. White. Pure. (*He does a take to audience.*)

PEARL. (*Looking like she is going to faint*) Oh my, you must forgive...(*She is starting to buckle.*)

(**JOHNNY** *catches her and helps her to the chair.*)

JOHNNY. I gotcha, ma'am. Here, let me help you. Why, you're trembling, and you must be cold and hungry too. Put this blanket around you.

(**JOHNNY** *grabs blanket on back of rocker and covers her.*)

Let me get my dear sweet mother and she'll fix ya some vittles. (*He calls offstage*) Ma. Ma. It's me, Johnny. Will you come in here, please? (*Looks at audience and smiles.*) I love milk, homemade apple pie, and (*Blushes*) my mother!

(*"Ta Da" music*)

MA. (*Offstage*) Yes, Johnny. I'll be right in. Let me finish fixin' dinner. I've to catch this hog, kill it, and gut it.

(*There is the sound of tires squealing and a thud like* **MA**'s *hit* it.)

MA. Gotcha. *(Hog squealing)* Hold still, ya little booger. *(Sound of something ripping)*

PEARL. Did I mention I don't do pork?

JOHNNY. Ma will be right in. Hmm, I wonder where my kid brother William is? You'll like William, ma'am. He is so good to our mother. Maybe he's upstairs. *(Yelling upstairs)* Hey little brother. William. You upstairs? Come on down, we got company. *(To* **PEARL***)* William is the smart one in the family.

(Loud manly footsteps are heard stage left slowly coming down the stairs. **BILLY** *enters stage left. His music is YMCA.* **BILLY** *is wearing a very typical western outfit: jeans, western shirt, boots, vest and a hot pink scarf around his neck.)*

BILLY. I've told you a hundred times. Don't call me William. It's Billy Boy.

JOHNNY. That's right. I'm sorry Willia…er, Billy Boy. We have company. This is Pearl Goldberg. I found her out in the storm and I've brought her here, so our mother could care for her.

BILLY. Oooh, where do you shop? Honey, we need to make a Von Maur run, and fast.

PEARL. How do you do, Billy?

*(***BILLY*** glares at her.)*

Eh, Billy Boy.

JOHNNY. Excuse me, I'll go see what's taking Ma so long.
*(***JOHNNY*** exits stage left.* **BILLY** *sits opposite* **PEARL** *and is appalled at her hair)*

BILLY. So tell me Pearl, who does your hair? Whirlpool?

PEARL. I know I must look a mess, but I've been walking for miles in this terrible snowstorm. I surely would have perished…

(By this time **BILLY** *is totally bored with her.)*

…if your broth…

BILLY. Yeah, yeah, yeah, so let's talk about me.

PEARL. Well, okay. I just thought…

BILLY. Do these jeans make me look too fat?

(**BILLY** *rises and turns.*)

PEARL. Eh? No. Anyway I was stranded...

BILLY. *(Very proud)* Like my booties. These boots are made from real ermine. They said they could make them out of beaver and I said..."Ooooo not on your life."

PEARL. Yes, they're very pretty, but...

BILLY. Have you ever been to a rodeo? I just love rodeos. All those bulls, and leather, and roping, and cowboys, and horses, and cowboys.

(*Hero Music.* **JOHNNY** *enters stage left, poses, and then is followed by his mother. Her music is "Home Sweet Home"*)

JOHNNY. Pearl ma'am, this is our sweet dear mother. Ma, this is Pearl Goldberg.

MA. Howdy, honey. My name is Opal Ringo. *(She shakes Pearl's hand vigorously.)* But you can jest call me Ma, like everybody else round here. (**MA** *spits on Johnny's boot.*) Pearl Goldberg huh? You ain't from around her, are ya?

PEARL. No, ma'am. My family is from Miami...Miami, Oklahoma.

MA. Well, ain't that nice. Well child, you look plum tuckered out...

BILLY. I'll say. I wouldn't wear that outfit to a tar and feathering. *(Thinks and smiles)* Ooooooh...feathers.

MA. Don't mind him, Pearl. He's my baby boy and sometimes he's just a little too cultured for us.

BILLY. Mother, I've told you a million times. You can't wear white after Labor Day.

JOHNNY. Well let's go into the kitchen and Ma will feed you the best vittles you ever et.

(*He helps* **PEARL** *up and they all see she is very pregnant-Mood music.* **MA** *gasps.*)

MA. *(Near tears)* Oh, Johnny. I can't believe you would do this to shame our family name. Bringing home a girl in this...*(Tragic music)* ...condition. *(Begins to weep)*

JOHNNY. *(Realizing what his mother must think)* Oh, no, Ma. It ain't what you think.

PEARL. Oh, no, Mrs. Ringo, it's not Johnny's baby.

(MA looks then at BILLY.)

BILLY. Yea. Right. Whatever.

JOHNNY. No, Ma. I've never met Pearl before tonight. I just brung her in from the storm.

MA. Oh, I'm sorry, son. I should have never doubted your purity. *(She hugs him and smiles.)*

BILLY. *(Stomping his foot)* What about my purity?

MA. *(Looking at BILLY and then out front)* So Pearl, you jest head on in and help yerself. We ain't too formal around here.

(PEARL exits stage left, followed by BILLY. MA starts to go to the kitchen but there is a knock at the front door. MA pulls JOHNNY downstage.)

MA. Son, that's probably the scumbag Judge Nasty coming by to laugh at us one more time before he throws us out. Don't let him git in yer craw. Remember I found Pa's last will and testament last night and he left us that gold mine in glorious Goddard. We'll leave this hole and start fresh. But Nasty musten know or he'll try to steal it fer sure.

JOHNNY. I know Ma, you can count on me.

(More knocking. BILLY enters stage right.)

BILLY. I'll get it. It's probably my Avon lady. She better have that hand cream. This prairie dust is ruining my pores.

(BILLY crosses to stage right, pulls out compact, and checks his hair.)

Come in.

(Villain music. JUDGE enters stage left.)

JUDGE. Good evening, friends. It's not a fit night out for man nor beast.

MA. And you'd be the beast, Judge REALLY Nasty.

JUDGE. Eh, That's Judge Riley Nasty. Now, now, my dear

Mrs. Ringo. You surely can't be holding a grudge this long, can you.

MA. You mean the fact that yesterday you foreclosed on this farm, torched our barn, stampeded our herd, shot my husband in the back and ran over our dog with your buckboard and killed him?

JUDGE. True, but I only meant to cripple that dog.

JOHNNY. I'm tellin you, Nasty. We ain't got no proof that you did all them things. And even if we did, yer also the judge in this territory so we ain't got a chance in your courtroom.

BILLY. Yes, and your posture is terrible too.

JUDGE. Can't we all just get along?

MA. You yella varmit. Me and my whole family will stand against you until the day we die.

(She moves right in front of **JUDGE**, *Music.* **JOHNNY** *stands right behind* **MA**. **BILLY** *pulls out a nail file and is doing nails and then he notices* **MA** *and* **JOHNNY**.*)*

BILLY. Oh!

(Startled, he skips and joins them. Music. But he continues his nails.)

JUDGE. Very well. But let me tell you this, you Kansas Trailer Trash.

MA. *(Very angry)* This is a mobile home. *(Stands erect, hands on hips, followed by* **JOHNNY** *and* **BILLY**)

JUDGE. Oh, forgive me. I couldn't tell when I drove up. The buckboard in the front yard on cinder blocks distracted me.

MA. Get to the point, you Oakie.

JOHNNY. Ma, there's no reason to get ugly.

JUDGE. *(Waving deed in their faces)* You got just 24 hours to leave this "mobile home," and I wouldn't stay in town neither, Johnny. Haysville ain't big enough for the two of us.

JOHNNY. Don't worry, Nasty. We're leaving in the morning. But someday I'll be back and you'll regret what you've done to the name of... *("Ta Da" music)* ...Ringo.

JUDGE. Oh, you're really scarin' me, Johnny Ringworm! Oh sorry, that's Johnny Ringo, isn't it?

JOHNNY. Why, you double dealin' no good polecat.

JUDGE. So, where ya movin'? To another shang'ra la like Kechi?

BILLY. No, smarty pants, for your information...

(**JOHNNY** *and* **MA** *are waving and trying to get* **BILLY** *to shut up.*)

...my daddy left us a big ole gold mine in Goddard and it's worth a fortune and we're gonna have more money than Cher and you'll be stuck here in this hillbilly town, cause you won't know we have it. *(He suddenly realizes what he's said.)*

Soup's on.

(**BILLY** *prances off to kitchen.*)

JUDGE. *(To* **MA***)* You must be so proud. Well, ta-ta, Ringos. I've got to go. It's been fun. Oh, Mrs. Ringo, when it comes to families, can you look up dysfunctional in the dictionary? *(Laughs)*

(**JUDGE** *exits. Villain Music.* **JUDGE** *re-enters.*)

JUDGE. Remember, 24 hours. *(Laughs and exits stage right)*

MA. Oh, Johnny, what are we gonna do now? Judge Nasty will surely try to get that map before we leave.

JOHNNY. Dear mother, don't you fret. Johnny Ringo won't let anything happen to this family.

("Ta Da" Music)

MA. Oh son, you're the glue that holds this family together, *(Sadly)* you're the reason I want to go on living without your Pa...that and the fact that I ain't looking to spend eternity with that sorry sack of...

JOHNNY. Ah shucks, Ma. I'm just doing what any loving son would do.

MA. But Johnny, how are we gonna get away from that villain?

JOHNNY. I got it, Ma. We'll take the wagon and head out

late tonight before he misses us.

MA. But son, you know this territory is swarming with wild Indians and what about poor pitiful pathetic pregnant Pearl? *(Hand extends and wipes her eyes.)*

JOHNNY. Ma, we ain't leavin' her behind. Nor the rest of her either. She's in trouble. The Ringos never turn their backs on anyone in trouble. We'll take her with us. And if need be, I'll marry that girl so that child will have a name. *("Ta Da" music)* And as for those Indians, remember we won blue ribbons in sharp shootin' at the Kansas State Fair.

MA. That's right. And Billy Boy won…for his pineapple souffle. Oh, Son. *(Very happy)* You make me so proud to be a Ringo. There's nothing about this family I'm not proud of.

(BILLY enters stage left wearing a pink cowboy hat and pink boots with a pink sweater tied around his neck. He is proud of himself.)

BILLY. Well, I'm dressed for dinner.

(Stomps off stage left as MA buries her head in Johnny's chest.)

(Blackout)

Scene 3

*(**AT RISE:** front of olio curtain)*

*(Villain music. **JUDGE** enters stage right and is in spotlight.)*

JUDGE. Now to lay plans to weasel that gold mine out of old lady Ringo and her two sons Johnny and Nelly Boy.

BILLY. *(Offstage)* That's Billy Boy.

JUDGE. But first, I'm going to need a little help. And the perfect foil will be my long-time servant, Ruby. Ruby Slippers.

*(Wizard of Oz Music. Spot hits stage left portal on the feet of **RUBY**. It slowly rises up until we see all of her. She is in a simple dress, but with ruby slippers).*

Ruby come here.

(Spot follows her to stage right.)

Have you changed the oil in the buckboard?

(She nods yes.)

Cleaned the outhouses?

(She nods yes.)

Scrubbed my underwear?

(She grimaces.)

Now listen, I want you to do exactly as I say…Wait a minute, is that a new dress?

(She looks puzzled and tries to speak.)

Oh, I forgot, you're a mute. *(Laughs again)* Oh Ruby, if only you owned a liquor store and had a flat head, you'd be a perfect catch for a wife. *(Laughs again)* Now listen you little waif. *(Hands her a note.)* Here's a message for Chief Smokincrack.

(Indian Music)

It lays out my ingenious plan to steal the gold mine from those low life Ringos. They're stupid enough to sneak out tonight and try and slip through the Indian Territory without Chief Smokincrack…

(Indian Music)

JUDGE. *(continued)* ...and his blood thirsty tribe finding out. But *(Indicating note)* this note will explain everything to ole Chiefy. So all I have to do is let them ambush the Ringos and get me that map. Of course, I'll share the gold mine with the Indians. I'll take the gold and give them the shaft. *(Laughs)*

(**RUBY** *shakes her head like, "No, don't do this."*)

And you can't warn them, because you can't read or write and you're a mute. This is perfect.

(**RUBY** *screams with laughter.* **JUDGE** *looks at her and she quickly covers her mouth.*)

Here, now take this to the Chief while I wait at the top of Mount Twin Peaks, or as the kids call it, Mount Hooters.

(**RUBY** *crosses back to stage left where* **CHIEF SMOKINCRACK** *is standing. Blackout stage right. Lights up stage left on* **CHIEF** *and* **RUBY**.)

CHIEF. Ruby Slippers, how come you here?

(**RUBY** *shows him the note.*)

Hmmmm, message from great white judge. Me call braves for pow wow.

(He waves a hand and two braves enter from stage left.)
Ruby, these me top braves: Greater Tuna.

TUNA. How.

CHIEF. And Little Beaver.

BEAVER. Chance.

CHIEF. Chance?

BEAVER. Yeah me know how, me want chance. (**BEAVER** *and* **TUNA** *howl and high five.*)

CHIEF. Shut up or me give you tomahawk chop.

(Braves get quiet.)

Let see what paper say. *(Reads note)* Chief Smokincrack. Me want you to attack Ringo wagon tonight. Me give you the secret signal from atop Mount Twin Peaks.

BRAVES. *(In unison and chest butting each other)* Mount Hooters.

CHIEF. You takem no prisoners. You Scalpem all white men. Big whompem for you if you do this. *(Looks at* **RUBY**) Hmmmmm me not know Judge speak em Indian. Ruby, you nice girl. Why you get mixed up with bad man like Nasty.

(She looks forlorn.)

Him speak with forked tongue. Old Indian saying, "Man who speak with forked tongue should not kiss balloon." *(When audience "boos," he reacts with:)* Hmmmm this em tough room. Ruby, see you at the massacre. Go Beaver and Tuna. You must ready braves.

*(***BEAVER*** and ***TUNA*** *exit stage left.* **CHIEF** *talks to* **RUBY:***)*

Me want them organized for war, not wanting them running round like a bunch of wild Indians. *(He laughs.)*

(Blackout)

Scene 4

*(**AT RISE:** Outdoor drop. Cut out Covered Wagon. Side view.* **PEARL** *and* **MA** *are drying the last of the dishes. The stage is dim light. Ominous Indian music is softly playing. Spot hits* **PEARL** *and* **MA** *and slowly goes up to Stage Right to Mount Hooters. We see* **JUDGE NASTY.**)

JUDGE. *(Laughing and wringing his hands, whispering to audience)* Shhh. Don't give me away, you want to ruin the storyline? Look down there. Those stupid Ringos are just sitting ducks. Speaking of ducks, it's time that Chief Smokencrack...

(Indian Music)

...gets down on those losers. *(Laughs)* I told you to be quiet. Now to give the secret signal to Chief Smokincrack.

(Indian Music. **JUDGE** *yells over the side.)*

Hey Smokencrack, they're down there. Attack now.

(Spot hits bar and we see all three Indians laughing and drinking.)

TUNA. So I says, "Come back to my tepee and I'll show you my etchings." *(All three laugh.)*

BEAVER. More firewater all around.

TUNA. So you know what kind of shirts Custer wore?

BEAVER. No, What?

TUNA. Arrow. *(All laugh.)*

(Spot picks up the **JUDGE** *again.)*

JUDGE. Hey, Abbott and Cochese. Are you going to the massacre or what?

CHIEF. Oh crap, I forgot. *(Indian accent is back)* Little Beaver take many braves up high road. Greater Tuna takem braves down low road.

(Braves start creeping through house.)

CHIEF. And me get to the massacre before ya. *(He screams.)*

(Blackout on stage right.)

(Lights come up on stage.)

MA. Pearl, honey, I wish you would go lay down in the wagon. You shouldn't be working in your condition.

PEARL. Now Ma, it's just drying dishes, besides we're done now.

(She goes into the wagon. Hero music. **JOHNNY** *enters stage right.)*

JOHNNY. Well Ma, the horses are tied up. I guess this is a good place to bed fer the night.

MA. I don't know, Johnny, I got a bad feelin' in my bones.

JOHNNY. Whattya mean, Ma?

MA. Something jes don't smell right.

*(***BILLY*** enters stage left.)*

BILLY. Woo, that's it, no more campfire beans for me.

MA. Do you think it's safe to stay here son? We're pretty close to Chief Smokincrack's camp.

(Indian drums)

JOHNNY. Don't worry Ma, we're at least 20 feet from there.

BILLY. Hey guys, I'm talking here.

(They look at him.)

Okay buckaroos, I'm gonna hit the sack. *(Hears the drums)* Hey, knock it off. Some of us cowpokes are trying to get some shuteye.

(Drums stop. **BILLY** *waves at* **MA** *and* **JOHNNY***)*

Night, night don't let the Gila monsters bite.

(He goes into the wagon.)

JOHNNY. Ma you go on to bed, I'll take the first watch. *(Drums start again)*

MA. Oh, son, be careful. Them devils are up to no good.

JOHNNY. It'll be okay, Ma. Nothin gets by...*("Ta Da" music)* ...Johnny Ringo.

(At that moment an arrow whizzes in front of **JOHNNY***'s face and he is oblivious. However,* **MA** *sees it and is frozen.)*

MA. Eh, Johnny, did you see that?

JOHNNY. See what, Ma?

(Another arrow shoots by his face.)

MA. Johnny, we're in big doo-doo.

JOHNNY. Naw, that's just Billy Boy.

MA. No Johnny, that was another arrow.

JOHNNY. Don't be silly Ma. I ain't seen no arrow.

(Another arrow shoots by him and the drums stop. **MA** *grabs really big thick glasses out of her bra and puts them on his face and shows him the arrow.)*

Holy crap. *(He yells.)* INDIANS. Take cover. Circle the wagons. *(He looks behind him.)* A...wagon. Ma, take cover.

*(***JOHNNY*** removes glasses and they take positions for the "Indians attacking" scene. Cowboy and Indians yell and shoot. Music is played throughout the scene.* **MA** *and* **JOHNNY** *take places at opposite ends of the wagon.* **CHIEF** *whoops by from stage left to stage right behind wagon.* **TUNA** *comes out of stage left to stage right.* **BEAVER** *comes out of stage right and goes to stage left. Braves are shooting arrows.* **CHIEF** *goes to run spotlight.* **TUNA** *is about to tomahawk* **MA.***)*

JOHNNY. Ma, look out behind you. *(***TUNA*** is shot by* **JOHNNY** *and falls off stage right.)*

MA. Johnny, I'm running low on bullets.

*(***BILLY*** comes out of the wagon dressed the same, except he is wearing a pink nightcap instead of his cowboy hat.)*

BILLY. Hey! Stop this massacre right now. There is a pregnant woman in there. *(He runs back into the wagon).*

MA. Billy, grab a gun an start shootin'.

JOHNNY. Yeah, we can use every man we can get.

BILLY. *(Sticks head out of wagon and smiles)* Me too.

MA. Johnny, look out.

*(***JOHNNY*** turns and sees* **BEAVER** *behind him.* **MA** *shoots and* **BEAVER** *falls offstage right.)*

JOHNNY. Thanks Ma, I owe ya one.

*(***BILLY*** comes out with an arrow in his hand and throws it at the Indians.)*

BILLY. Stop shooting those arrows.

(He prances back into wagon. **TUNA** *comes out stage left and shoots* **MA** *in the chest with an arrow. She yells and clutches her chest.)*

MA. I'm hit. *(Yells into wagon.)* I'm coming in. Pearl cover me.

*(***PEARL*** jumps out of the wagon with two pistols blazing and bullets crisscrossing her chest, a cowboy hat on and big cigar in her mouth. She is yelling and shooting.)*

PEARL. Come and get me, you dirty savages. You want a piece of this? You lily livered louts? *(She heads back into wagon.)*

BILLY. *(Coming out of wagon)* Well I hope you're happy. My souffle just fell.

(He stomps back into the wagon. **MA** *Reappears with a crutch and a bloody, bandaged head. She is firing her pistol.)*

MA. Pearl, quick get inside the wagon.

*(***PEARL*** goes in.)*

JOHNNY. Ma, you're hurt.

MA. Naw son, it's just a flesh wound.

*(***BILLY*** reappears with arrow in hand.)*

BILLY. Stop it! I mean it. This is all fun and games until someone loses an eye.

(He goes back into the wagon. Music stops. Blackout on stage. Spot hits **JUDGE**. *He has two pom-poms.)*

JUDGE. Back…Pack…Smokencrack. Shoot You. Back…Pack…Smokencrack Shoot You.

(This is done to the cheer of Rock Chalk KU. Blackout on **JUDGE**. *Lights and sound resume on stage.)*

JOHNNY. Ma, I'm out of ammo.

MA. Me too.

JOHNNY. Looks like it's hand-to-hand combat, Ma. Me and Billy will hold them off. You go take care of Pearl!

*(***BILLY*** comes out of the wagon with a white flag and runs around and screams.)*

BILLY. Help. Help. Don't hurt me. I'm a bleeder. Take the women.

(BILLY runs off stage right.)

JOHNNY. Save yourself Ma, take Pearl and head for the hills.

MA. Not on yer life. *(To Indians:)* Bring it on, Smokencrack. Let's kick butt, son.

(MA takes a fight position. Next is a series of tableaus. Stage right is MA and BEAVER. Stage left is JOHNNY and TUNA. Loft on JUDGE. Stage left on BILLY quaffing his hair. Spotlight hits PEARL centerstage.)

PEARL. Now where's their chief, that coward Smokencrack? *(Indian Music. Stage lights come on and sound track fades out.)*

CHIEF. *(At spotlight)* I'm at the spotlight.

PEARL. What the hell are you doin up there?

(We see JOHNNY and MA peeking out from stage left and stage right to see CHIEF.)

CHIEF. *(He is coming down to the stage.)* Well, somebody has to run the spot at this cheapass theatre. I've got to sell the tickets, play a vital role in this show, run the spotlight. *(He bangs on ladies restroom door)* Hey lady, hurry up in there. I've got to clean those toilets in ten minutes. And who do you think pops all this popcorn? The popcorn fairy?. And for what? Minimum wage and one lousy shift drink? I can't take it anymore.

(He cries.)

MA. *(Consoling him)* Oh, it's okay.

(Villain music. JUDGE enters stage right holding a gun.)

JUDGE. Oh grow up you baby. Now nobody move.

(He grabs BILLY and puts gun to his head.)

Or Fluffy gets it.

BILLY. *(Squeals)* Wait. I thought the bad guy always takes the young pretty girl, not the young pretty boy. **(JUDGE** *is thinking.)* And a pregnant girl is even better. Just think, two hostages in one.

JUDGE. You're right. Come here.

*(He pushes **BILLY** away for **PEARL**.)*

BILLY. *(Perturbed)* Bossy boots.

JOHNNY. Billy, I can't believe you did that.

BILLY. Well I'm sorry, but I have a hair appointment in ten minutes with Mr. Rudy and you can't just walk in. I had to call weeks ago...

JUDGE. Shut up. Now Ringo, hand over that deed.

JOHNNY. *(Takes deed from shirt)* You've got the upper hand now Nasty, but you've not seen the last of Johnny Ringo.

("Ta Da" Music)

CHIEF. Good work Judge. You sharem gold with Chief.

JUDGE. Yea sure Chief, right after...Joan Rivers stops with the face lifts.

CHIEF. You cheatem Chief?

*(**CHIEF** crosses to **JUDGE** when **TUNA** sneaks behind **JUDGE** and takes his gun. **CHIEF** grabs deed Then **JOHNNY**. Then **TUNA**. Then **PEARL**. Then **JUDGE**. **JUDGE** then exits stage left and runs around backstage to come stage right. He is followed by **MA**, **BILLY**, **TUNA**, **JOHNNY**, and **CHIEF**. Slowly followed by **PEARL**. **JUDGE** enters and stops stage left and puts deed down shirt. **CHIEF**, **JOHNNY**, **BILLY**, and **MA** tickle him and try to get it. **JUDGE** is laughing hysterically. Finally **MA** gets it, crosses to stage right and puts it down her blouse. All run to her and tickle her to get it. **BILLY** gets it and runs stage right and puts down his pants. All look and are disgusted with the idea of retrieving it. **JUDGE** and **CHIEF** sneak off stage right and cross back stage left so they can come out of stage right.)*

PEARL. I ain't proud, come here Tinkerbell.

*(She crosses from stage right to stage left and is groping **BILLY** as he is screaming. She finally gets the deed. She proudly holds it above her head.)*

Ha! Ha!

(**CHIEF** *comes out of stage left and grabs the deed from* **PEARL**.)

CHIEF. Ho! Ho!

(**JUDGE** *comes out of stage left and grabs it*)

JUDGE. He! He!

(*He runs out of stage left and runs around backstage followed by everyone but* **PEARL**. *She rests at piano bench.* **JUDGE** *enters stage right and runs across the stage and grabs* **PEARL**.)

Don't try to follow me or you know what will happen?

BILLY. What?

(**JUDGE** *sighs and drags* **PEARL** *through Stage left.*)

JOHNNY. (*To audience*) If it's the last thing I do, I'll bring Pearl back to the loving arms of my Ma.

(*"Ta Da" Music*)

BILLY. (*To audience*) Me too! (*Poses*)

(*YMCA music.* **RUBY** *enters from stage left. Wizard of Oz Music. Titanic Theme as* **RUBY** *and* **JOHNNY** *see each other.*)

JOHNNY. Oh be still my heart. Who is this gem of loveliness out here in the middle of nowhere? I'm the king of the world.

CHIEF. This Ruby Slippers. She work for that scumbag, Judge Nasty.

JOHNNY. I don't believe it. How could she? She's so innocent. Dear lady please tell me this can't be true.

(**RUBY** *smiles and looks dumbfounded.*)

CHIEF. Ruby servant to Nasty. She no talkem. She mutem.

MA. Oh, you poor baby. Johnny, I thinks she likes you.

JOHNNY. (*Embarrassed*) Oh, Ma.

(**RUBY** *tries to tell them about* **JUDGE** *with sign language, but they are clueless. Finally she realizes she must do charades instead.*)

MA. Johnny, she's trying to tell you something.

CHIEF. Maybe she tellem us though charades. (*They all look at him with shock.*) We Indians, not heathens you know.

MA. Yes child, show us what you mean through charades.
BILLY. Oh, I love charades. Chiefy, you can be on my team.
(**RUBY** *starts out by showing five fingers.*)
CHIEF. How.
(**RUBY** *looks disgusted.*)
JOHNNY. No, that means 5 words.
BILLY. Wait, is it a movie or a book?
MA. Billy Boy, it's a problem.
CHIEF. What sign for problem.
JOHNNY. Shhh she's doing something.
(**RUBY** *mimes "Judge Nasty has taken fat girl to his cabin up on Mount Hooters. Help me to get free from his clutches." **RUBY** gestures using a gavel.*)
MA. Hammering.
CHIEF. She building tepee.
JOHNNY. No it's a gavel. Judge?
(**RUBY** *nods pleasingly. Gestures Dirty Dancing.*)
CHIEF. War dance.
MA. It's some kind of a dance.
BILLY. Oh my God. It's *Dirty Dancing*. I love Patrick Swayze. He's so nasty.
(**RUBY** *points to her nose, nodding, "yes that's it."*)
JOHNNY. Judge Nasty. It's Judge Nasty.
MA. What about him, honey?
(**RUBY** *does a gesture like pulling a rope.*)
MA. Oh, he has done something.
CHIEF. What Ruby, speak up.
(**RUBY** *changes and tries taking a penny out of her hand.*)
JOHNNY. She's begging.
MA. No she's cupping her hand.
BILLY. Judge Nasty wears a C cup.
CHIEF. This takem too long.
(**RUBY** *points to her nose.*)
JOHNNY. That's it. Take. Judge Nasty takes…

(**RUBY** *walks like a pregnant girl and holds hands out.*)

JOHNNY. Something about a bad back.

MA. Oh, it's a duck.

BILLY. It's a duck with a bad back.

JOHNNY. No. No. She means the fat girl. Judge Nasty takes fat girl...go on.

(**RUBY** *holds up two fingers.*)

BILLY. The peace sign. I got it. Judge Nasty and the fat girl have joined Greenpeace.

(*Everyone is stunned.*)

MA. No. Two. Judge Nasty has taken Pearl to...go ahead Ruby.

BILLY. Dillards? Von Maur? Banana Republic?

(**RUBY** *charades a cabin.*)

CHIEF. Box?

MA. Door?

BILLY. Lemon Pledge.

JOHNNY. House?

(**RUBY** *wants more info*)

MA. Cabin. Judge Nasty has taken Pearl to his cabin.

JOHNNY. Ruby, quick, where is the cabin located?

(**RUBY** *points to the top of her head.*)

CHIEF. Hair.

MA. Head.

BILLY. Silly putty? I hate this game.

JOHNNY. Top? Judge Nasty has taken Pearl to his cabin at the top of... ?

(**RUBY** *mimes getting on a horse.*)

MA. Jumping.

CHIEF. Horse.

BILLY. The home shopping network?

JOHNNY. Mount. Judge Nasty has taken Pearl to his cabin at the top of Mount?

(**RUBY** *motions breasts. Stoops down they're so heavy.*)

MA. Hunchback?

(RUBY stands erect.)

CHIEF. Hunchfront?

BILLY. Anna Nicole Smith.

MA. Down? Bring the curtain down.

(It does, to everyone's surprise.)

JOHNNY. No, I got it. Judge Nasty has taken Pearl to his cabin at the top of Mount Hooters.

(RUBY points to her nose and near collapses from exhaustion. All applaud.)

BILLY. I said that ten minutes ago and no one would listen.

JOHNNY. Chief we have to join forces to bring down Judge Nasty. If you help us, we'll share the gold mine profits with you and your tribe. You can use the money to educate your children.

MA. And improve your housing.

JOHNNY. Better transportation.

CHIEF. Hell, we're opening a casino.

(Whoops off stage right and everyone follows.)
(Blackout)

Scene 5

(Inside the cabin of Judge Nasty. Pearl is tied and gagged in a chair. Judge is reading deed at the table.)

JUDGE. *(Villain music)* So the gold mine is in Goddard. *(Looks at the audience)* Oh well, I'll live anywhere for money. *(Pearl tries to talk.)* Speak up dear. Hankerchief got your tongue? *(Laughs)*

JOHNNY. *(Hero Music. Enters room from stage right with gun out)* Hold it right there Judge. Untie that woman. *("Ta Da" Music. Judge holds up his hands.)*

JUDGE. You wouldn't shoot an unarmed man would you Ringo? Let's fight this out like men. *(Ringo puts gun on table and Judge pulls one out of his belt.)* You hillbilly crackhead. Now you're gonna get it.

MA. *(Enters stage left behind Judge.)* I wouldn't try that hombre. Mamma's got an itchy trigger finger. Now gimme that gun.

JUDGE. *(He does.)* You got me Mother Ringo. But just one thing Is bothern me.

MA. What's that Judge?

JUDGE. Why is there a big bear behind you? *(She screams and turns and he pulls a gun out of his pocket.)* Now turn around slowly you hillbilly deadbeat. *(She does. He takes her gun.)* Now you Ringo, get over here with your old lady. *(He does.)* Now I kill two Ringos with one bullet. *(Laughs)*

CHIEF. *(Enters Stage right with arrow in Judges back.)* Hold it Right there Nasty or you'll be a Sioux City Shishkabob. *(Chief takes his gun.)*

JUDGE. *(He turns to face him.)* I get the point Chief. Can't we talk this out? I mean we been bad guys together a long time.

CHIEF. Yea until you tried to swindle me too.

JUDGE. Look I'll tell you what. Oh look free firewater. *(Chief turns and smiles. Judge gets another gun out of his hat)* hands up you hillbilly Indian. You two get over there with Chief Really Stupid. *(They do.)* Now its four of you hicks that will never see another flea market again. *(He aims gun at MA)* And you're first Ma. *(JOHNNY moves around so he's behind MA.)*

BILLY. *(Enters from stage left behind JUDGE and puts a hair dryer in his back.)* Okay one false move and I'll blow you away. *(He laughs at his own joke. To audience.)* Get it? Now turn around Mr. Man. *(During all this PEARL is up and down with pleasure and disgust at this fiasco.)*

JUDGE. Billy Boy. Well if you don't look hot. Is that a new outfit?

BILLY. *(Pleased and flattered)* I got it for a Mardi Gras party_ I'm going to next week. *(He lowers his hair dryer. Judge pull another gun from MA's bra.)* Do you really like it?

JUDGE. All right, don't move your hillbilly hair dresser. So now I've got the whole fam damily. *(Laughs)* Hey, Princess Grace over here, get with the rest of the royal family.

(RUBY enters stage right and puts a broom stick to the JUDGE's back.)

JUDGE. How many people did you bring?

JOHNNY. Just enough to bring you to justice, Judge. Good work Ruby.

JUDGE. *(Turns quickly)* Ruby. So this is the way you repay me for treating you so well. Giving you great threads to wear. All the rice cakes you want.

JOHNNY. Ma untie Pearl.

(She does.)

MA. She is already.

PEARL. You got here just in time. Judge spilled his guts to me and I know the reason why poor Ruby can't speak.

BILLY. Of course stupid. She's a mute.

PEARL. Quiet, Nelly Bell. Anyway it's the slippers. They were once owned by a wicked witch from way out west.

JUDGE. Actually they were my mothers.

PEARL. Those shoes have a curse and anyone who wears

them can't talk. *(All look at shoes then to* **BILLY** *who is primping again.)* Anyway, Ruby remove those slippers and you'll be a free, talking, shopping, nagging woman again.

BILLY. Does she have to click them three times or anything?

(Wizard music. **RUBY** *removes shoes and everyone is holding their breath. Johnny takes her in his arms.)*

JOHNNY. Oh, Ruby, I love you and now you're free to say the same. You do love me, Ruby. Don't you?

RUBY. *(Her voice comes from a man, who is offstage)* Yes, Darling. I've loved you since we first met. Kiss me you big galout. *(They kiss.)*

MA. Oh I just love a happy ending.

RUBY. Me too Mother Ringo. But what about Pearl?

PEARL. What about me?

RUBY. I just thought Johnny was the father…

PEARL. Oh no. Ruby. The real father is oH..oh..

MA. What is it Pearl?

PEARL. It's time.

BILLY. About 10:15

MA. No you idiot. It's time for the baby.

BILLY. Well, I don't know nothing 'bout berthin no babies either. *(**MA** slaps **BILLY** three times.)*

RUBY. Quick, Johnny, help her into the wagon.

MA. Billy, you boil some water.

BILLY. Great. I could use some hot tea right now.

(He exits stage left. **MA** *and* **JOHNNY** *help* **PEARL** *off stage right.)*

CHIEF. Me get bullet for squaw to bite on.

*(**CHIEF** exits stage left.)*

RUBY. Now it's just you and me, Judge Nasty.

JUDGE. Now Ruby. It was just a harmless prank.

RUBY. *(Picks up gun.)* Put em on Nasty.

(He puts on shoes as best he can.)

Hurry up you swine. Now dance, eh I mean talk.

(He gulps and then tries. **RUBY** *smiles. "Sounds of silence" music)*

RUBY. Ah, the sounds of silence. *(She laughs. Suddenly we hear a baby cry.* **JOHNNY** *pushes* **PEARL** *out in a wheelchair. She is holding the baby.)*

BILLY. *(Re-enters)* Oh it's the baby. I'm doing the baby shower.

RUBY. Pearl what is it.

BILLY. Well da, it's a baby.

PEARL. It's a baby girl. And her name is Leah. Leah Rae. Because she's my ray of sunshine. *(***BILLY*** wails)*

MA. Now, Pearl, it don't make any difference to us, but I have to solve this mystery. May I ask the baby something?

("Who's your Daddy" song sung by **MA***)*

MA. Well Pearl who is it?

(These are all freeze frames. Spots hits **JOHNNY** *and* **RUBY**. *Then* **GREATER TUNA**. *Then* **PIANO PLAYER**. *Then* **BEAVER**. *Then* **JUDGE** *and finally* **BILLY**. *During all this* **PEARL** *brings up a man from the audience. Spot hits them.)*

PEARL. Leah, here's your daddy.

(And reprise of song begins. Bows.)

The End

ANOTHER KENNEDY IN THE WHITE HOUSE

or

THIS AIN'T CAMELOT

by
Tom Frye

For
Kennedy Marie Frye

CAST

JACK B. NIMBLE –Our trusty and handsome farmer
JILL KENNEDY – Our dainty and really stupid heroine
RODNEY DANGERFIELDMOUSE – A tall teller of tails
BUTTERLIPS – A cow who milks the audience for laughs
GEORGE W. BUSHWACKER – President of United Dates of America

ANOTHER KENNEDY IN THE WHITE HOUSE was first presented by Patty Reeder and Scott Noah at Mosley Street Melodramas, Wichita, KS., June 20, 2007. Lights and Sound by Marty Gilbert, props by Amy Saker, musical direction by Susan Cato, costumes by Patty Reeder and choreography by Tom Frye. It was under the direction of Tom Frye. It ran for 6 performances.

CAST
(In Order of Appearance)

RODNEY DANGERFIELDMOUSE .... Scott Noah
JACK B. NIMBLE .... Tony Hayes
JILL KENNEDY .... Sarah Frazier
PRESIDENT GEORGE W. BUSHWACKER .... Tom Frye
BUTTERLIPS .... Tom Frye & Scott Noah

SYNOPSIS OF SCENES

Diddley, Kansas 1800's

Scene I (In front of the curtain)
Scene II (Jack's farm)
Scene nI (A street in Diddley, Kansas)
Scene IV (Bushwacher's office)
Scene V (A street in Diddley, Kansas)
Scene VI (Kentucky BaUcap Racetrack)

Scene 1

*(**AT RISE:** Opens with spotlight hitting the loft. We see a large rat head and his two hands. He is wearing a necktie. He is speaking a la Rodney Dangerfield....)*

RODNEY. Hello and good day to you all. You're probably asking yourself, "So who's the big rat?" Well, my name is Rodney Dangerfieldmouse and I'm going to tell you all about the melodrama you're about to see. It's called "Another Kennedy in the White House or This Ain't Camelot." Don't let the title fool you. It's not full of political jokes–besides, political jokes usually get elected.

(Beat)

Come on folks, I laughed when you came in. I tell you, with this crowd, I get no respect. Take my cheese... please. Anyway, I'm the narrator or story teller. Also as I said, I'm a rat. Now that's not to be confused with a dinner theatre producer. That's a lower life form. Anyway, I digress. So this tale...

(His tail flies over the proscenium and hangs.)

Not that kind of a tale. Sorry kids, that's my own tail.
(His tail goes back.)

This tale is spelled T-A-L-E, not T-A-I-L. This tale or story if you will, takes place on a farm outside of Diddley, Kansas. Now don't confuse that with Diddley-squat, Oklahoma or Bo Diddley or Bo Derek or Bo Bo the dog face boy from the Kansas State Fair.

(He thinks a second)

Wait a minute, that's Jo Jo the dog face boy. Anyway, you see that curtain down there with the ladies painted on it? That's called the olio curtain. Well it's also a magic curtain. It won't go up unless you say the magic words. And I, Rodney the Rat, am the only one who knows the magic words. So if I tell you the magic words, then the curtain will go up and we can get on with this tale.

(His tail flies over again.)

Sorry my tail has a mind of it's own. Okay, now listen carefully to the magic words. There once was a man from Nantucket. No wait, that's another story. Oh yeah, I remember how it goes: Pow chicka pow pow. Now you all say it with me.

(The audience all repeats it.)

RODNEY. *(cont'd)* Hey, that was great. I'm finally getting the respect I deserve. But we're not done yet. It doesn't work unless we add a little neck action. Here, I'll show you.

(He sways his head back and forth as he says:)

Pow chicka pow pow. Now you all try it.

(The audience repeat with him.)

Now there's only one thing left to do. We all do it again and then when we finish saying it, we point our hands to the curtain, wiggle our hands and say, WOO. Got it? Pow chicka pow pow and then point, wiggle and woo. Alright let's do it together.

(The audience does and the curtain rises.)

You folks are wonderful and that's not a tall tale.

(A very long stiff tail rises behind him, very slowly.)

Tall tale, get it? Man, this is a tough room. I tell ya, I get no respect. As you can see, it was a hot day in Diddley, Kansas. It was so hot...

(He waits for audience to say " How hot was it"?)

It was so hot, the chickens were laying fried eggs. Fried eggs, get it. *(He laughs.)* Sorry, folks, that joke was really foul. Foul! I'm killin me. *(He laughs again.)* Boy, can I really shell 'em out. *(Laughs again)* Shell 'em out, get the yoke? *(Laughs and there is a telephone ring)* Man that's probably Comedy Central calling now. *(Yells backstage)* Tell them to call my agent.

(Beat)

So let's introduce our main characters again just to see if you remember them. First, our dashing hero, Jack B. Nimble.

(HERO *enters and poses.)*

RODNEY. *(continued)* They wanted me to play the hero, but I was out of town during casting. I told them I was in Maize. They said, "Oh, you're in Maize, Kansas"? I said, "No, I'm a rat, I was in a maze." *(Laughs and hits microphone)* Is this thing on? Now our lovely heroine.

(**JILL** *enters and poses.*)

Wow, what a babe. I really wanted to date her, but my life is already such a rat race. And now for our final character, and I do mean character, our villain.

(**W. BUSHMACKER** *enters.*)

Nice booing. It's nice to see that someone else gets no respect. Alright, you guys clear the stage so we can begin this tale. *(Tail flies over)* Geeze!

(**RODNEY** *does a double take to himself.*)

Did somebody say cheese?

(**RODNEY** *exits*)

Scene 2

(**NOTE:** *This scene is played in an area spot SR or SL.*)

(**JACK** *enters SL with milk pail and sings most of, "Oh, What a Beautiful Morning." When he gets to a little brown maverick who is winkin her eye, a cow head pops from SR. It is* **BUTTERLIPS.**)

JACK. There you are, Butterlips.

BUTTERLIPS. Good morning, Jack.

JACK. My, it's a glorious, brisk, and chilly morning. Are you ready for your morning milking? *(She nods and he starts to go around to milk.)* I'll get started.

BUTTERLIPS. Eh, eh, eh. I don't think so. *(He looks puzzled.)* Aren't we forgetting something? It's really cold this morning, Jack.

JACK. *(He looks at his hands.)* Oh, sorry, Butterlips, I almost forgot.

(**JACK** *pulls gloves from back pocket and puts them on and then goes to start milking behind portal. We hear milking sounds and it turns into a waterfall of sound effects as cow does take.* **JACK** *comes back with the pale.*)

Wow, Butterlips, you out did yourself today.

BUTTERLIPS. Anything for you, Jack. I know the rent is due soon and the more milk money you make, the easier it will be to pay Mr. Bushwacker.

JACK. Good ol' Butterlips. You're the best milk cow in the world.

BUTTERLIPS. Thank you, Jack. You make me so happy too. Let's sing my favorite song.

JACK. Good idea, maybe that will put me in a good mood.

(**JACK** *sings the "Moo Cow Song" from Gypsy.*)

JACK. Thanks, Butterlips. I'm in a great mood now. I'll just mosley on into town and talk to President Bushwacker and see if he'll extend my rent payment.

BUTTERLIPS. Good luck, Jack.

(**JACK** *exits.*)

BUTTERLIPS. *(continued)* He's gonna have utter failure.

Scene 3

(**SETTING:** *A street in Diddley, Kansas.*)

JACK. Holy cow patties, I'll never get enough money to pay Mr. Bushwacker. My life is really spiraling downward. I'll become a bum. I'm liable to end up working for some cheezy melodrama company. To top it off, there's no single attractive woman in all of Diddley. The only available woman in this town looks like a cross between Rosie O'Donnell and a prune.

(JILL *appears on the opposite side of the stage. He is awestruck.*)

Holy raging hormones, who's she? She's the most beautiful woman I've ever seen. She must be an import from the hottie town of Eastborough. My heart is bursting with love. I must meet her. But I must not let her know how I feel. I must be cool, suave, and debonair. That's it, act like Bill Clinton.

JILL. Hello there.

(JACK *turns to jelly physically and begins to blabber.*)

JACK. Blab, blab, blab. (*He ends with his tongue hanging out*).

JILL. You seem to have dropped something (*She pushes his tongue back in his mouth and wipes off his drool.*)

JACK. (*To audience:*) Wow, she's a girl. (*To* JILL:) We don't get many girls out this way, Ma'am. Are you new in town?

JILL. Why yes, I just moved to Diddley. I came from Doo Dah, Kansas. You know where that is, don't you?

JACK. Oh, sure. Isn't that the town that has been working on Kellogg for 73 years?

JILL. Yes, and in 40 more years, it will be completed. Anyway my name is Jill, what's yours?

JACK. My name is Jack B. Nimble.

JILL. Ohhhhh, Jack and Jill.

JACK. Jill, it's such a fetching name.

JILL. It only pales to Jack.

JACK. So, Jill, you headed up the hill?

JILL. Well, I was, but I came tumbling down to the corner

drug store. You see, I've got a little pickle in my throat.

JACK. Don't you mean tickle?

JILL. No, pickle. You see after I brush my teeth, I always have to take some mouthwash and gerkin. *(She make gargling sounds.)*

JACK. Gerkin? Don't you mean gergle, I mean gargle.

JILL. No you gargle with a tickle and you gerkin with a pickle. Anyway some people say there's a frog in my throat, but that sounds too ribbeting. Besides, if I don't get some medicine soon, I could croak.

JACK. Then you'd really be in a pickle.

JILL. Yes, and I'm concerned I could lose my voice. You see, I use to sing for a living. But alas, I had to stop.

JACK. Why did you stop singing?

JILL. On account of my voice teacher Mr. Finklesnort. He said I hit the L note.

JACK. The L note?

JILL. Yes one day in my lesson, I was really singing high and he said it sounded like– (**JACK** *cuts her off.*)

JACK. Oh yes, I think I understand.

JILL. You know once before I lost my voice. I was singing Beethoven's Sunlight Contata.

JACK. You mean Moonlight Sontata.

JILL. Oh no, he wrote this one during the day. So there I am singing Beethoven's Sunlight Contata and Mr. Finklesnort yells, "Stop!"

JACK. He stopped you in mid-Sunlight?

JILL. Yes and he immediately told me what the problem was, so I ran into the kitchen.

JACK. You lost your voice and you ran into the kitchen?

JILL. Yes, and my voice was, right behind the stove.

JACK. Right behind the stove?

JILL. Well of course it was, because Mr. Finklesnort said it was out of my range.

JACK. *(Repeats with her)* Out of your range.

JILL. Say, how does my voice sound now? Can you hear me?

(She begins mouthing. No words come out and then finally...)

JACK. Oh my goodness, I can't hear you at all.

JILL. Sometimes only dogs can hear me.

JACK. Lucky for us, not so lucky for the dogs.

JILL. What?

JACK. Nothing.

JILL. You know once I had a dog. He was a mixed pedigree.

JACK. Mixed pedigree huh?

JILL. Yes, 50% Lab retriever, 50% Poodle, and 50% Che Who-a Who-a.

JACK. Che Who-a Who-What?

JILL. Che Who-a Who-a. You know, them little Mexican hairless dogs without any hair?

JACK. No hair, huh? They'll save a lot on combs.

JILL. Oh that's silly, dogs don't use combs!

JACK. I'll try to get back on track.

JILL. You already missed the train. Anyway, you know how some dogs fetch sticks? Well this dog fetches tacos and burritos. He was so cute and so was his twin brother.

JACK. This Che Who-a Who-a had a twin brother?

JILL. Oh yes, and I named my little Che Who-a Who-a José. And guess what we named his twin brother?

JACK. What?

JILL. Hose B.

JACK. Of course you did. Now aren't these the little bitty dogs that sit in tea cups?

JILL. Not my José. He was a big dog. He was so big... .

JACK. I'll bite, how big was he?

JILL. He weighed over 200 pounds.

JACK. That big?

JILL. Oh yes, and I took him over to the vet when he got sick.

JACK. He got sick, huh?

JILL. Oh my, yes! He got something lodged in his throat.

So we took him to my vet, Dr. Charlie Horse. So the Doc picks him up in his arms and took one look in his mouth and decides he's going to have to put poor José down.

JACK. Oh no, he had to put him to sleep.

JILL. No, he had to put him down. I told you he was heavy. Now can we talk about something I want to talk about?

JACK. Well, certainly. What do you want to talk about?

JILL. My family. Let's talk about my sister Vincent.

JACK. You have a sister named Vincent?

JILL. Oh yes, and she only has one ear.

JACK. She wasn't a painter by any chance, was she?

JILL. For goodness sake! How did you know?

JACK. Lucky guess.

JILL. She was the world's most famous paint-by-number artist in Haysville.

JACK. My that's quite an honor.

JILL. Oh, you have no idea. Parades, opening super markets, kissing babies, bowling, peach picking.

JACK. Peach picking?

JILL. You've never been to Haysville, have you?

JACK. *(Shakes his head)* No.

JILL. But sadly she had to give up painting. Medical condition.

JACK. Oh I'm sorry to hear that. Were her eyes going bad?

JILL. Yes, she just couldn't see the numbers anymore.

JACK. Well, why didn't you get her glasses?

JILL. Oh we did, but with one ear, they kept falling off.

JACK. They kept falling off. Yes. Well, it's certainly been an experience...Miss?

JILL. Kennedy.

JACK. Well, Miss Kennedy, you certainly make my heart sing ("A You're Adorable" duet!) Gee, Miss Kennedy, I hope we will see each other again.

JILL. Well, maybe so. I'm going over the the United Dates of America Office, so maybe we'll be on each other's date list. Do you know the address?

JACK. Why yes, it's the big white house on the corner. 1600 Pennsylvania Ave. I'm going there too. The President of the United Dates of America, George W. Bushwacker is my slumlord, er, landlord, and the rent is due on my farm. I need to talk to him. May I walk you over?

JILL. I would love that, Jack.

(They exit.)

Scene 4

(**SETTING:** *Oval Office of* **GEORGE W. BUSHWACKER** (**GW**). *"Hail to the Chief" is playing.*)

GW. Entree vous, wilkommen, come on in.

JACK. Hello, Mr. Bushwacker. Thank you for seeing me. I've come to ask you for a favor.

GW. Sure. What do you want, chocolate, strawberry or vanilla?

JACK. Not flavor, sir. Favor.

GW. Oh, sorry, my hearing is going.

JACK. Beg pardon?

GW. Never mind, Doofus, what do you want? Dad's waiting for me on the golf course.

JACK. Well, it seems we've had a small problem on my farm. We had a plague of locust...

GW. Oh really? Gee, I hope they haven't eaten all your crops, devastated your land, and ruined your income for the year.

JACK. Well, Sir, that's exactly what they've done.

GW. Oh, Jack, that breaks my heart. I need a moment to be sorrowful. *(Bites knuckles so briefly)* Times up, now where were we? Oh, yes, so where is my rent payment?

JACK. That's just it, G.W.

GW. Eh, that's President Bushwacker, Jake.

JACK. That's Jack, President Bullwinkle.

GW. Bushwacker, Jerk.

JACK. Not Jerk, Mr. Tushwasher.

GW. Bushwacker, Bushwacker, Bushwacker!

JACK. Yes, Sir, Mr. Bushwacker, Bushwacker, Bushwacker.

GW. *(Begins crying on his desk.)* I didn't wanted this job. Dad pushed me into it. All I wanted to be was a vote counter in Florida, but, no! My brother Nub got that job.

JACK. So anyway, since I lost my crops and I don't have one red cent to my name, could I get an extension on my farm rent until next year?

GW. Not on your hanging chad, Bucko.

JACK. But sir, if I can't pay you, then what will become of my farm?

GW. I don't know, maybe I'll build an amusement park. I'll call it, "Bushwacker Gardens", or "Six Flags over George."

JACK. Oh, please don't do that, you'll put *(Insert local amusement park)* out of business.

GW. Too late. Anyway, what do I care? You owe me $150 and it must be paid by noon tomorrow and if you don't pay, then it's the unemployment line for you. Now get out of my office before I call homeland security.

JACK. Yes, Sir. But there's someone else who wants to see you.

GW. Is that Kerry guy trying to move in. He just won't give up will he?

JACK. No, this is a lady. Her name is Miss Kennedy and she's wanting to find a date through your dating service. I thought maybe you could hook her up with a... let's see...a farmer, about 6', handsome. Do you know anyone who fits that description, Mr. President?

GW. No. Now get out.

(JACK exits and then JILL knocks. GW starts primping.)
Come on in.

JILL. *(Entering)* You must be Mr. Bushleague.

GW. Bushwacker.

JILL. I'm so pleased to meet you. I hope you can find me a date.

GW. Well, please be seated, Miss Kennedy. Now, first I must ask you a few preliminary questions. First of all, what are you looking for in a man?

JILL. Breathing.

GW. Well, that eliminates Dick Cheney. How about his salary?

JILL. Oh, whatever vegetable he eats is okay with me.

GW. No, not celery! Salary - his paycheck.

JILL. Oh, that's not important. All I care about is that he treats me nice.

GW. Well, well, well. Let's see what the computer has to say. (**GW** *crosses to a machine with a large wheel on it. He puts the paper in a slot.*)

JILL. Gee, a computer, I didn't think those would be invented for years.

GW. Yes, I know, but this computer is in the early stages of development. *(He goes to desk intercom.)* Yes, Miss Rice? Would you send in the materials to start the computer?

(**RODNEY** *enters and walks over to wheel and starts to spin it.*)

Faster, Rat, faster.

(**RODNEY** *looks angry and spins faster as the computer lights up and spits out a piece of paper.* **GW** *picks it up and crosses to* **JILL**. **RODNEY** *stops and is out of breath.*)

That'll be all, Rat.

RODNEY. Al Gore gets more respect than me.

(**RODNEY** *exits.*)

GW. Well, my dear, the computer says that the man of your dreams is very close.

JILL. Gee, really? How close?

GW. Oh *(He moves closer to her.)* About 3 inches away.

JILL. Wonderful. Will you move out of the way so I can see him?

(**GW** *starts to move.*)

GW. It's me, you Pumpkin Head. Eh, I mean, you Darling Girl!

JILL. Has that machine been oiled lately?

GW. Yes, it's quite up to date, my dear.

JILL. Can I demand a recount?

GW. *(Yelling)* No more recounts. *(Catching himself)* You see the machine never lies. So it looks like you've found your man.

(**GW** *starts to kiss* **JILL** *and she moves away.*)

What is it my dear? Where are you going?

JILL. I'm not sure I can trust a big rat in this white house

GW. Now, now, let's not get personal. Oh! You mean that big rat. Well, I assure you everything is above board and kosher.

JILL. Do you gerkin to?

GW. What? Listen Miss Kennedy, let's not waste any time. Let's set the wedding date right now. Let me check my calendar. *(He goes to desk)* Hmmm, not tomorrow, it's golf all day. How about some day next week? No can do, it's a full week of $1000-a-plate dinners...any day the last two weeks of the month? Darn, it's more vacationing and golfing with Dad. Gee I don't get back to the White House until April 2007, and maybe not even then. How about late June?

JILL. Well, let me check my calendar.

(She pulls out a book and looks quickly and slams it.)

Sorry, full up and can't marry you until never.

GW. What does this mean, you little snip? I'm a man of power and money and you will marry me and become first lady of this dating service. Or else!

JILL. Or else what? You have no power over me. I want a real husband, one who will treat me like a lady and take me off to Camelot and we'll live happily ever after.

GW. Don't hold your breath, Toots. *(He starts to move in towards her.)* Come here you little tart.

*(**GW** grabs her puts her arm behind her back as she screams. **JACK**, hearing her screams, enters to save her.)*

JACK. Unhand that lady, you cad.

GW. Me? Oh, sorry I was just helping her unkink her arm.

JILL. *(Running to **JACK**)* Oh Jack, you saved me from a fate worse than death.

JACK. Someone was going to make you watch reruns of "Three's Company" again?

JILL. No, not that bad. Mr. Bushwacker was making

advances.

JACK. Shouldn't he do that at the bank?

JILL. Never mind, let's just get out of here.

GW. Just a moment you two. Remember you've got til noon tomorrow to come up with the $150 bucks or it's out in the streets for you. However, Miss Kennedy, you are welcome to stay. There's an internship available here at the White House.

JILL. Are you crazy? I'd rather die or choke to death on a beret. Oh Jack, come on, we'll figure out a way to come up with that money before tomorrow.

JACK. Good day to you sir, Mr. President.

(*JACK and JILL are exiting as he mutters:*)

Gee, his office looked more rectangular than oval.

GW. (*Laughing*) Very well, you two! Just you wait until tomorrow and you'll see the wrath of G.W. Bushwacker!

(*Curtain falls.*)

Scene 5

*(**SETTING**: Street scene in Diddley, Kansas)*

JACK. Well, Jill. It looks like we're in deep water now. How in the world will be come up with $150 by tomorrow noon?

JILL. It's always best to be calm and think things through when in trouble.

*(**RODNEY** has entered SL with a newspaper.)*

RODNEY. Psst..psst.

JILL. Is there a leak somewhere?

RODNEY. Hey over here.

JACK. Hey who are you?

RODNEY. *(Acting very suspicious and with sunglasses on.)* My name is Rodney and I work in the office of G.W. Bushwacker. I've got some inside information for you. It's all very secret.

JILL. I thought I smelled a rat.

RODNEY. Look living in the sewer ain't no bed of roses.

JACK. No, she meant that we thought something was a little shady with our Mr. Bushwacker.

RODNEY. Well listen carefully. I know that tomorrow at the Kentucky Ballcap…

JACK. Don't you mean Kentucky Derby?

RODNEY. Naw, this horse race ain't quite so fancy. Anyway I know that GW has a horse entered that's gonna make him rich.

JILL. What's this horse's name?

RODNEY. Paul Revere.

JILL. So what does that have to do with us?

RODNEY. Well, this horse is being ridden by G.W. himself and he's going to win and first prize is $10,000.

JILL. Wow. $10,000 if you won that, you could pay off that $150 you owe and have $850 left over.

RODNEY. Hmmm, she ain't the brightest bulb in the lamp is she?

JACK. Are you kidding? She flunked her SAT's.

RODNEY. How can you do that?

JACK. When she filled out the application, she couldn't spell SAT.

RODNEY Okay, look Einstein. The race is rigged. G.W. has paid off the jockeys of the other two horses. They're going to throw the race. Hold their nags back so he can win.

JILL. But that's cheating.

JACK. Right on the ball again.

RODNEY. But I know a way to change all that. The other two jockeys are riding Valentine and Epitaph. So tomorrow before the race we slip in and you and Jill change places with the two jockeys and you, Jack, ride to the finish line and win that $10,000.

JACK. What's the name of my horse again? Valentine?

JILL. And I'll ride Epitaph.

RODNEY. That's right. And G.W. will Ride Paul Revere. *(He breaks into song with the other two.)*

Fugue For Tin Horns

Scene V

(***SETTING:*** *a racetrack, in front of Olio.*)

(**RODNEY** *is up on the loft again. He has a microphone and binoculars as he is doing the play by play of the horse race.*)

RODNEY. Good morning racing fans! Here we are at the Kentucky Ballcap. Yes, the dash for the dandelions. Today's race is a hot one. And now let's go down to the race track and see those nags. (*Looks at lady in audience.*) No, not you lady. Now here comes the first horse. Epitaph ridden by the great jockey Jackie Gleason.

(**JILL** *enters SL riding a stick horse with a racing cap on a colored jacket and half mask. She parades across the stage and off SR.*)

Next we have the long shot Valentine. He is being ridden by his jockey Orson Welles.

(*Enter* **JACK** *on stick horse and does the same parade. He also has a half mask.*)

And last our favorite Paul Revere being ridden by G.W. Bushwacker. Let's give all these fleabags a hand. And may the best horse win and the worst end up at the glue factory. But first a message from our sponsor.

(*Beat*)

The House of Wong. That's right The House of Wong serving famous Chinese dishes for over 50 years. Their specialty is Mouse a Tongue (*Points to his own tongue*) Get it? Mouse a tongue. I tell you, I get no respect! All right the horse are lined up at the starting gate.

(*We hear the starting bell.*)

And they're off.

(*Each horse enters through the SL portal and races across the front of the stage and exits the SR portal and goes back around again.*)

It looks our favorite has jumped out front.

(**GW** *comes on and runs across stage. He is followed by* **JACK** *and then* **JILL**. *Each is about ten foot behind the other riding their stick horses.*)

RODNEY. *(cont'd)* And here they come rounding the last half mile.
(They re-enter with JILL, then GW, then JACK.)
It looks like our heroine is leading by a neck, followed by our nasty villain. Just a length behind is our hero.
(They exit and come around again and now this is all done in slow motion from SL to SR.)
Wait! Our hero is moving up, he's passing the villain and is breathing down the neck of our heroine. She doesn't seem to mind however. The pressure must be too much as she is falling behind. Now our hero has the lead all by himself, the villain has suddenly burst into second place leaving our heroine to bring up the rear. Boy, does she has an edge in that department.
(JILL shoots RODNEY a glare.)
Now they're heading for the back stretch. It's Jack, then G.W. then Jill, no wait, Jill has moved into second and G.W. is in last. Jill is overtaking Jack and G.W. is moving back to second and Jack is falling behind. Wait, Jack has a sudden burst of speed as he is neck and neck with G.W. Now they both are moving in on Jill. This is incredible folks! They are neck and neck and neck. Boy, that's a lot of neckin' for a G-rated show. They're approaching the finish line and there they go past the the finish line. Oh my gosh! It's a photo finish!
(They all run through the SR portal and olio rises again as they all three enter the room with photographs in their hands.)

JILL. Oh this one is great. Look at your nose, it's right there on the line.

GW. Yes, that's nice, but my hair was messed up.

JACK. Naw...you look great. But look here in mine, I've got those red eyes.

JILL. Oh don't worry, I know someone who can alter that and fix them.

GW. Really? Could he make me taller?

RODNEY. *(Entering behind them)* Hey, Hey. Can we just get back to the show?

GW. Yes, where's my winner's trophy?

RODNEY. Sorry, G.W. But as you can clearly see here in the photo finish. The winner is Epitaph.

GW. What? But these two losers were suppose to lose this race.

JILL. *(Taking her mask off)* Yes, but I'm not a loser and I won. So I want that prize money.

GW. You? How did you get on that horse?

RODNEY. Well, I persuaded your other two jockeys to let Jack and Jill ride instead. *(He hands **JILL** a wad of money.)* Here's your winnings.

GW. But how? Those two are my trusted cabinet members.

RODNEY. It seems the ship is sinking and they are all jumping ship like a bunch of rats. And trust me, I know.

JACK. *(Taking his mask off)* So Mr. President, you are foiled again.

GW. Who's the dummy now?

JACK. What do you mean?

GW. You didn't win the race. Jill did. She gets the money not you. And you're the one that owes me $150. And it's ten seconds 'till noon. So if you don't pay up, then I take your farm. *(He laughs.)*

JILL. Not so fast G.W. *(She turns to **JACK**.)* Here, Jack. Here's all the money. Now you can pay him off.

JACK. Here, you villain! Now never darken our door way again.

*(**GW** slinks off.)*

But Jill you didn't have to give me all the money, I just needed $150. You've got $10,000.

JILL. It's okay, once we're married, I'll get it all back anyway. *(She hugs him.)*

JACK. Ohh! Caught like a rat in a trap.

RODNEY. Please, that's not very P.C.

The End

From the Reviews of
THE MOSLEY STREET MELODRAMAS VOLUME I ...

"*The Lost Samantha Treasure* is nothing if not memorable - and hysterical. Frye has certainly penned a good one this time around, tossing some of the more well-used melodrama jokes out the window in favor of a humor that requires timing and talent.
- Sharon Faith Levin, *Wichita Old Town Gazette*

"...Melodrama fans are happily cheering it again. *The Lost Samantha Treasure* is terrific fare for the whole family."
- Jacqueline Boudreau, *Wichita Old Town Gazette*

"Like most modern melodrama scripts, Frye's *Samantha* is pretty much just a vehicle for slapstick silliness, but the dialogue in this one is darned funny...Frye had a blast...the d'enouement...features Saturday Night Fever - style dance numbers. The audience certainly enjoyed watching the show the evening I attended.
- Terri Mott, *F5 Newspaper*

www.ingramcontent.com/pod-product-compliance
Lightning Source LLC
Chambersburg PA
CBHW070833300426
44111CB00014B/2536